ENDURING IDEAS
Contributions to Australian Debates

Gabriël A Moens AM

Published in 2020 by Connor Court Publishing Pty Ltd

Copyright © Gabriël A Moens 2020

All rights reserved. No part of this book may be reproduced or transmitted in any form or by any means, electronic or mechanical, including photo copying, recording or by any information storage and retrieval system, without prior permission in writing from the publisher.

Connor Court Publishing Pty Ltd
PO Box 7257
Redland Bay QLD 4165
sales@connorcourt.com
www.connorcourt.com
Phone 0497-900-685

Printed in Australia

ISBN: 9781922449252

Front cover design: Maria Giordano

Front cover picture: Jan van Goyen (1596–1656)
Jan van Goyen: View of a Village on a River, wikimedia commons.

I dedicate this book to Dr Edith Moens, who has accompanied me on a lifetime journey of scholarship and discovery.

This book is also dedicated to scholars who have facilitated the development of my academic career and have influenced my thinking on legal, social and political issues. They include Professor Ilmar Tammelo, Professor Julius Stone, Professor Alice Ehr-Soon, and Professor Lauchlan Chipman and many other people who, although they did not have an academic position, stimulated my intellectual curiosity with their common sense and entrepreneurial flair.

CONTENTS

Preface 7

1 Enduring Ideas: The Intellectual Landscape of this Collection 11

2 On Civil Disobedience 19

3 Values Clarification Courses in Australian Schools: A Parent's View 31

4 The International Protection of Minorities: An Individual or a Group Approach? 43

5 Honouring the Contribution of Mothers to the Family: A Letter Exploring the Proper Role of a Catholic University. 53

6 Speech to Celebrate the National Civic Council's 50th Anniversary 59

7 An Assessment of Australian Education 69

8 Reflections on an American Sabbatical: Diversity and Free Speech 83

9 The New Ethnic Consciousness: A National Language Policy for a Multicultural Australia? 105

10 Ralph McInerny and the Authority of the Pope: A Response to a Lecture 121

11 Our Free Australian Society: Promise or Reality? 127

12 How to Mismanage Organisations 143

13 The Contribution of "The Christian Foundations of the Common Law" to Enduring Ideas 159

14 The Protection of Public Health: Reflections on the Covid-19 Pandemic and the Role of the State 171

15 Nederlands: De taal van de gemiste kansen (Dutch: The Language of Missed Opportunities) 191

About the Author 204

PREFACE

This sample of Professor Gabriël Moens' contributions to Australian debates over the last 40 years aptly demonstrates the enduring nature and importance of his ideas. This contribution shows no sign of dissipating as his challenging 2020 reflections on the Covid-19 pandemic and the role of the State evidence (Chapter Fourteen). History will ultimately judge whether Australia learns anything of enduring benefit from the experience of this pandemic, but this volume will be at least one tangible consequence. As Professor Moens explains in Chapter One of this book, it was his forced confinement to his home during the Great Lockdown that lead him to revisit and assemble the works here collated. The recovery of these works, important previously but difficult if not impossible to find, will expose both the original readers and a new audience, many of whom were born after some of these works were written, to the wisdom of Professor Moens. This is a cause for gratitude and celebration.

The volume is not just a record of a life well spent which is of value as an historical artifact. It is an opportunity to apply a lifetime of learning and careful analysis to contemporary, and no doubt future, challenges to our nation and to the world. This is because the issues which Professor Moens grapples with here are human issues which may disappear from public consciousness for a time but regularly re-emerge for consideration over and again: the legitimacy of civil disobedience (Chapter Two), parental concerns over mandated content in schools (Chapter Three), the protection of minorities (Chapter Four), the proper role of Catholic Universities (Chapter Five), Australian education (Chapter Seven), diversity and free speech (Chapter Eight), multiculturalism (Chapter Nine), the Authority of the Pope (Chapter Ten), the extent to which Australian society is properly characterised as free (Chapter Eleven), management of organisations (Chapter Twelve) and the importance of Christianity to Australia (Chapter Thirteen).

It is hard to believe that Professor Moens wrote the following words forty years ago: "It could be argued that a system does not function adequately anymore when some groups have entrenched power positions in society and use their power to impose their will on weaker or vulnerable classes of people." When these words were written who could have imagined an Australia in which the free exercise of speech, conscience and of religious belief would be overridden so frequently by Australia's governments. At that time there was no *Abortion Law Reform Act* 2008 (Vic) and its counterparts in Queensland and the Northern Territory had not been passed. These provisions require medical practitioners with a conscientious objection to abortion to participate in that procedure by providing a referral to patients seeking it. They led to the investigation of Dr Mark Hobart for his unwillingness to refer a couple who wished to obtain a termination of a 19-week pregnancy on sex-selection grounds. The same Victorian legislation first introduced exclusion zones in Australia. They now also exist in the Australian Capital Territory, Northern Territory, Victoria, Tasmania, Queensland and in New South Wales. *The Public Health Amendment (Safe Access to Reproductive Health Clinics) Act 2018* (NSW), for example, created an exclusion zone of 150m and prohibits, among other things, making communications in relation to abortion that are reasonably likely to cause anxiety or distress to any person accessing, leaving, or inside an abortion facility. Under this regime "sidewalk counselling" is criminalised. To discuss alternatives to abortion and offer practical assistance such as free medical care or housing in the zone is now an offence punishable by a $5,500 fine or 6 months imprisonment for a first offence with double the penalties for a second offence. These are very significant penalties for expressing views contrary to those of the lawmakers and evidence a system that "does not function adequately anymore."

Similarly, Professor Moens' 1989 concerns about the loss of respect for parental rights in the education of children speaks powerfully to a contemporary audience: "We should always ask ourselves by what authority schools and teachers take away from parents the responsibility for the general upbringing of their children. It is appropriate, then, that we should reaffirm that parents are and remain the primary educators in the areas of values and attitudes about family life, roles, and behaviour."

Professor Moens may have been writing about the recent imbroglio which lead to the rejection by some universities of funding for a program on Western civilisation with these words from his 1992 piece on Australian education: "The reading of the great writers of Western civilisation is now seen as an imposition and as culturally discriminatory."

In his 2018 paper Professor Moens observed that, "It is important to mention that the Western world has itself weakened its ability to protect the Christian foundations of the common law. This is because the West has progressively devalued the importance and the role of religion in Western society."

Professor Moens is not afraid to express his position unambiguously and strongly. He can clearly see a society which is becoming increasingly unmoored from its roots and he is able to pinpoint some of the consequences. This is refreshing. Not every reader will agree with everything said in this book and that was certainly not Professor Moens' objective in writing the papers it collates. Some will, for example, not share his concerns about the current abridgement of civil rights and the rule of law during the COVID-19 pandemic. It is hard however to disagree with his conclusion that, "It will be interesting to see how the Covid-19 crisis unfolds and what the lasting consequences will be for the protection of citizens' civil rights and the rule of law in Australia. But there is no doubt that Nanny has triumphed!"

One thing is certain: this volume will at least cause a reaction in most readers, affirmation by some but not all. I am sure that, given his commitment to freedom of religion, conscience and speech, Professor Moens would welcome robust criticism as well as enthusiastic acclaim for this work. I encourage you to read this book and ponder the enduring ideas it discusses.

Professor Michael Quinlan
Dean and Professor of Law
The University of Notre Dame Australia, Sydney
15 May 2020

1

ENDURING IDEAS: THE INTELLECTUAL LANDSCAPE OF THIS COLLECTION
(2020)

When writing this Introductory Chapter, the world is in the menacing and deadly grip of Covid-19, better known as the Coronavirus. People arriving from overseas are placed in quarantine and many are compulsorily accommodated in hotels around the country for 14 days or are required to self-isolate. The borders of the States and Territories have effectively closed and people, especially people over 70, are encouraged or ordered to stay at home. It is a pandemic that has brought the best and the worst out of people. A Care Army was formed in Queensland to perform chores, like shopping, that older and vulnerable people seek to avoid. But we have also seen the ugly television pictures of people fighting in the aisles of our stores to buy toilet paper.

As I am confined to my home office, I had time to look at my dusty files which go back about four decades. I found 30 papers and speeches, written in the 90s (and even earlier) and the early part of this century, which have never been published completely. Upon re-reading these papers, I discovered that they deal with many issues and themes which are still relevant today. It is fascinating to read papers that have been written some 30 years ago, yet deal with current issues still debated in contemporary Australia. I have collected twelve of these papers to publish them as a book entitled *Enduring Ideas: Contributions to Australian Debates*. I have also added three more recent papers that deal with current topical issues.

I have kept the papers as they were written at the time of writing, only correcting obvious grammar and spelling mistakes. The number of footnotes has been kept to a minimum. Nevertheless, in some cases, I have added a few footnotes which, in most cases, did not appear in the original manuscripts which were often meant to be delivered orally to an audience. In doing so, I have endeavoured to clarify some of the issues discussed in the papers. Specifically, from time to time, I have added a footnote to alert readers to any legislative measure or judicial development that, since writing these papers, have addressed the issues under consideration.

The papers are in chronological order with the only exceptions this Introductory Chapter and Chapter Fifteen, a Dutch-language paper, the English-language title of which is *Dutch: The Language of Missed Opportunities*. The papers in this Collection deal with several Australian debates of the 80s and 90s, including but not limited to, the right to resist an unjust law, values clarification courses in schools, the contributions of mothers to the family, the protection of minorities, the authority of the Pope, free speech, diversity, the role of education, freedom of religion, affirmative action and multiculturalism, the role of the State to protect peoples' health, ethnicity and the mismanagement of organisations.

One of the acrimonious debates that took place in Australia from the 60s to the 80s involved the right of people to disobey valid laws. This debate, which was presumably nurtured by Australia's involvement in the Vietnam war, spawned an avalanche of papers on the concept of "civil disobedience". My mentor, Professor Ilmar Tammelo, published an article entitled *How should we react to unjust law?* on Monday, 10 August 1970 in the Sydney Morning Herald. Dr D G Boland responded in the Sydney Morning Herald on Saturday, 29 August 1970 with a paper entitled *Right of a lawbreaker*, which in turn, was commented upon by Dr Otto Bondy. The Australian Society of Legal Philosophy (ASLP) devoted several meetings to the issue of civil disobedience. Specifically, Haim A Cohn, in 1968, contributed a paper to the ASLP on *The Right and Duty of Resistance*. Upendra Baxi, also in 1968, addressed *The sociological aspects of the right to resist*. Arthur Kaufmann, at the same meeting, contributed on *Martin Luther King: Reflections on the Right to Resist*. René Marcic who tragically died in an air crash in Belgium on 2 October 1971, presented a paper to the ASLP on *The Right to Resist as an Attribute of Human Dignity*. R N Watterson contributed a paper to the ASLP in 1974, entitled *An Enquiry into the meaning of civil disobedience* with a comment by Lyndel V Prott. When I arrived in Australia on 1 January 1975, this debate prodded me to reflect on the concept of civil disobedience. The reflections published in this Collection were written in 1979 or 1980.

My involvement with the National Civic Council (NCC) in the early part of the 90s resulted in an invitation to speak at the Council's 50th Anniversary celebration in Brisbane in 1994. An abridged version of my paper on the NCC's 50th Anniversary Celebration was subsequently published in the *National Observer* (Australia's leading independent current affairs quarterly) in No. 80, Autumn 2009, 47-52 under the title *B.A. Santamaria's contribution to Australia's culture wars*; it is also based on a speech I delivered at the inauguration of the B.A. Santamaria Library, Cloverdale, Perth on 10 June 2009. But the version, here published as Chapter Six, is the original paper from 1994.

Several papers in this Collection deal with Australian education. In the late 80s and early 90s, I regularly spoke at meetings of the NCC in Queensland and New South Wales. Often, I addressed what I believed was a malaise in Australia's education system. On 24 September 1989 I addressed a community forum in Inverell about *The Humanistic Tide: The New Intolerance*. Some of my reflections on Humanism are incorporated in Chapter Three of this Collection which provides a parent's view on the introduction of Values Clarification courses in Australian schools. Chapter Seven focuses in general on the quality of Australian education and laments the demise of the teaching of grammar in high schools and universities.

I spent the first half of 1991 at the University of Notre Dame, South Bend, Indiana. My sabbatical provided me with an opportunity to focus on the concepts of "diversity" and "free speech" which were heatedly discussed in the United States and in Australia at that time. My office at Notre Dame was opposite the office of Professor Douglas Kmiec, who presented an unsuccessful proposal to the University Senate to honour the contribution of mothers to the family. I wrote a Letter supporting the proposal and, in this context, I reflected on the proper role of a Catholic University. This Letter appears as Chapter Five in this Collection. At Notre Dame, I also contributed to a Conference on *The Right of Ethnic Minorities* held on 28 February1991. My paper on *The International Protection of Minorities: An Individual or Group Approach* is included in this Collection as Chapter Four. The Collection also contains a paper in which I reflect, in general, on my American sabbatical. Specifically, Chapter Eight focusses on the concepts of "diversity" and "free speech". Sometime later, when I had returned to the

University of Queensland, a Professor of Philosophy of Notre Dame, Ralph McInerny, gave a public lecture at the University. I was fortunate to be asked to respond to his lecture; my response which focuses on the authority of the Pope is reproduced in this Collection as Chapter Ten. At the T C Beirne School of Law of the University of Queensland, I taught Constitutional Law. As such I was often asked by community organisations to speak about the Commonwealth Constitution. Chapter Eleven, entitled *Our Free Australian Society: Promise or Reality?* is one of the papers that I presented throughout Queensland.

One of the major debates in Australia in the 80s and 90s focussed on "ethnicity" and "multiculturalism" and the claim that Australia should develop a Language Policy for a Multicultural Australia. Being "ethnic" myself, I was interested in this debate and wanted to contribute to it. I read with interest the most interesting papers on "multiculturalism" published by the late Professor Lauchlan Chipman in *Quadrant* and other journals. I learned a great deal from Professor Chipman, and it encouraged me to contribute a paper, here reproduced as Chapter Nine, on *The New Ethnic Consciousness: A National Language Policy for a Multicultural Australia?*

I have always been interested in the theoretical and practical aspects of management. Throughout my career I have been able to observe the mismanagement by managers of their organisations and the failure to inspire employees. When I was Dean of Law and Pro Vice-Chancellor, I was determined to avoid the many horrible mistakes made by "managers". I realised that it is not unusual for employees to allege that the organisations for which they work are mismanaged. Even if these allegations are unsupported, the fact that they are raised regularly justifies an examination of how organisations may be mismanaged. This examination, reproduced as Chapter Twelve, focuses on actions or practices by senior management which may potentially result in the mismanagement of their organisations. In particular, it identifies three management practices which, in my experience, constitute "mismanagement": (a) the appointment of managers to their level of incompetence which, in turn, may lead to occupational stress and low staff morale, (b) the appointment of employees who are deemed to be less "intelligent" than, or "inferior" to, the appointers, (c) the centralisation of resources which requires constant restructuring and associated change management. A different version of Chapter Twelve has previously been published under the title "How to Mismanage Organisations: A Lawyer's Perspective" in vol. 1, No 1, Jan 2015, *Global Journal of Business and Social Science Review*, 2015, 1-10. This paper was immensely influential and has been quoted regularly throughout the world. I offer the audience the original, shorter version of this paper, with minor modifications, for their appreciation.

As I have always been interested in the interplay between Law and Religion, I was thrilled when Professor Augusto Zimmermann asked me to write the Preface to his three excellent books on *The Christian Foundations of the Common Law* published By Connor Court Publishing in 2018. I was also asked to launch Volume III in Brisbane. In my speech, which is reproduced as Chapter Thirteen, I concentrate on the relevance and importance of religion in Australia.

As I have observed earlier, at the time of writing, we are in the grip of the Covid-19 virus pandemic. To defeat the virus, the Government arrogated far-reaching powers to itself and adopted several controversial restrictive measures to protect the health of its citizens; these measures are economically punishing and seriously affect the civil rights of people. In this context, it is appropriate in Chapter Fourteen to consider the role of the State in the protection of public health.

Chapter Fifteen is, perhaps unusually, written in the Dutch language. I have long pondered the suitability of including a Dutch-language paper in this Collection, considering that most people would not be able to read it. However, I decided to include the paper for the following reasons. First, it was written for, and delivered orally at, a meeting of the Federation of Netherlands Societies Ltd in Sydney some 40 years ago. The paper, which explored the "ethnicity" of Dutch-speaking people was very well received and, for many years, was a resource used by the Dutch community in Australia, and in the presentation of the Dutch-language programme on Radio 2EA of the Special Broadcasting Service. Second, I argue in this paper that the Dutch language could have been a world language, like English, but it failed to take advantage of the opportunities which presented themselves during the last five hundred years or so. Although I do not address the role that the Dutch language played in the development of Australia, a reading of the paper certainly goads readers into a reflection on the lost opportunities of the Dutch language in Australia. Indeed, "New Holland" was the name given by Dutch sailor, Abel Tasman, to Australia in 1644. However, New Holland was never settled by the Dutch people and, hence, an opportunity to introduce the Dutch language and culture was lost. The Dutch language is a language of missed opportunities.

I invite my readers to now embark on a journey of reflection, involving the discovery of ideas and arguments which, at least in a small way, have contributed to the making of Australia.

2

ON CIVIL DISOBEDIENCE
(1980)

1. The International Covenant on Civil and Political Rights and Civil Disobedience

The International Covenant on Civil and Political Rights (Covenant) does not mention the concept of "civil disobedience". Nevertheless, an investigation into the meaning of this concept is necessary because it may be argued that, at least, some acts of civil disobedience are protected by paragraph 2 of Article 19 of the Covenant according to which "Everyone shall have the right to freedom of expression" and paragraph 2 of Article 18 which stipulates that, "Everyone shall have the right to freedom of thought, conscience and religion." Such argument may take one of two forms. First, it may be argued that some acts of civil disobedience constitute what has become known in the constitutional law literature as "symbolic speech". Second, the argument may be made that the exercise of the rights to freedom of thought, conscience and religion implies the right of a person to breach any law which is incompatible with these rights. If any one of these two arguments were valid, then the Australian Human Rights Commission or similar human rights body would need to establish Guidelines to enable prospective practitioners of disobedience to distinguish between "protected" and "unprotected" acts of civil disobedience. It is the aim of this paper to clarify the need for some Guidelines and to comment on their nature. The establishment of such Guidelines necessitates an enquiry into the concept of civil disobedience and into its role in society. Therefore, it is appropriate to briefly discuss the meaning of "civil disobedience" in the next part of this paper.

2. Attempts to define "civil disobedience"

The Australian and American involvement in the Vietnam war spawned a voluminous literature on the concept of, and justification for, civil disobedience. Whilst most writers emphasise the need to clarify the concept of civil disobedience, their writings on the subject have not resulted in a generally acceptable definition. Indeed, despite its popular use, many definitions of the term "civil disobedience" are contradictory and mutually exclusive. Nevertheless, it is possible to establish minimal requirements without which an act could hardly qualify as civil disobedience. First, "civil disobedience" is described generally by legal philosophers as a deliberate violation of a valid law, namely a law which is promulgated in accordance with the formal requirements of a legal system. Second, a lawbreaker breaches a valid law because it is incompatible with "higher" principles, for example, moral or religious dictates.

The first essential requirement of civil disobedience, namely that it involves a deliberate violation of a valid law, presents us with conceptual problems which may be clarified with an American example. In the United States, courts have the power to determine the constitutionality and, consequently, the validity of laws which have been passed by the legislature. If a law is declared unconstitutional following its deliberate breach by a lawbreaker, then the question arises whether this breach is described appropriately as an act of civil disobedience. I submit that the deliberate violation of a law prior to its being declared unconstitutional may qualify as civil disobedience for the following reasons. The reasons which induce a lawbreaker to disobey the law may be different from those which convince the court of its unconstitutionality and, hence, the reasons offered by the lawbreaker do not necessarily coincide with the reasons advanced by the courts. But even if the reasons which are advanced by a lawbreaker and the reasons given for the unconstitutionality of a law coincide, the act would still be properly referred to as "civil disobedience". This is so because a valid law remains legally valid until a court declares that it is unconstitutional. Assume that a violator breaks a valid law because it is, in his or her opinion, in conflict with the freedom of expression guarantee of the Covenant. If that law were later declared by a court as incompatible with this guarantee, then the lawbreaker's reasons and the reasons of the court would coincide.

A brief survey of American literature dealing with human rights reveals immediately the importance of this issue. For example, in the fifties, American civil rights leaders deliberately violated the segregation laws of the southern States. Is it proper to describe these protests as acts of civil disobedience in the light of *Brown v Board of Education*[1] which declared that separate education is inherently unequal? *Brown* was followed by many Supreme Court decisions which declared segregation a violation of the Fourteenth Amendment to the United States Constitution which reads, in part, "nor shall any State deny to any person within its jurisdiction the equal protection of the laws."

The second requirement envisages that the lawbreaker acts because the impugned law is arguably incompatible with "higher"

---

1   347 US 483 (1954).

principles, for example, moral or religious principles which are considered superior to the violated, yet valid, law. This requirement that a breach of a valid law should be based on "higher" principles is a necessary element of a minimal definition of civil disobedience because it enables us to distinguish between an act of civil disobedience and a criminal act. A criminal act also involves a deliberate violation of a valid law, but the violation is not usually based on a higher principle but is motivated by self-interest. However, a sharp distinction between an act of civil disobedience and a criminal act cannot always be made easily because the satisfaction of one's self-interest could be regarded by the perpetrator as a moral principle which is superior to the violated law. Hence, the two requirements of a minimal definition of civil disobedience are not always enough to distinguish an act of civil disobedience from a criminal act. Therefore, it becomes necessary to introduce a third essential element of a satisfactory definition, namely the "purpose" of violating a valid law.

A discretionary violation of valid laws does not qualify as civil disobedience because an act must aim at bringing about social change. The act of civil disobedience is the means used by a lawbreaker to expose what he or she considers as intolerable injustices existing in society. The eagerness to expose injustices also implies that the act of civil disobedience is performed publicly. The public nature of an act demonstrates that a law is not breached for reasons of self-interest, thereby obviating the need, in most cases, to treat the breach as a purely criminal act. Also, acts of civil disobedience could go on forever without being challenged if they are not performed openly and publicly. In such case, the value of the acts would be questionable because their impact on society would not be known.

The question whether an act of civil disobedience should be

non-violent in character is debated heatedly in the relevant literature. Although some writers agree that civil disobedience should be non-violent in nature, it could be argued reasonably that there are some instances of societal injustice which could be remedied only through violent means. I do not intend to settle this dispute with finality because it is unlikely that general agreement on the meaning of the term "violence" could be obtained. Also, a discussion as to whether acts of civil disobedience should be non-violent assumes that non-violent means of expressing dissatisfaction with a specific law meaningfully exists in society. Some scholars would argue that the very nature of modern society and its manifestations, for example a distorted education or entrenched economic power, are simply subtle form of "violence".

Professor Carl Cohen makes a distinction between direct and indirect forms of disobedience.[2] Direct disobedience involves a breach of the valid law itself which is deemed to be incompatible with "higher principles". Indirect disobedience involves the violation of a valid law which is not (or is only indirectly) related to the object of protest. An example of direct disobedience is provided by the infamous case of *Plessy v Ferguson*[3] which introduced the "separate, but equal" concept in American constitutional law. Plessy, who was of seven-eighths Caucasian and on-eight African blood, purchased a train ticket to travel from New Orleans to Covington. Upon entering a coach reserved for whites, he was ordered to sit in the coach reserved for coloured people. He refused and was arrested. He was subsequently charged with violating a Louisiana statute passed in 1890 which provided for separate but equal facilities for blacks and whites. Thus, Plessy disobeyed a law which was the very law against which the protest was directed. An example of in-

---

2   Carl Cohen, "Civil Disobedience and the Law", 21(1) *Rutgers Law Review*, Autumn 1966, 4-5.
3   163 US 537 (1896).

direct disobedience would be the deliberate violation of a trespass law to object to the intention of the government to make discrimination against homosexual people illegal. The distinction between direct and indirect civil disobedience is not academic only because, as I will argue later, the latter is usually much harder to justify than the former. In other words, the distinction facilitates the process of justification of specific acts of civil disobedience.

Is civil disobedience compatible with Section 2 of Article 18 of the Covenant according to which "Everyone shall have the right to freedom of thought, conscience and religion"? It is argued by some scholars that this Article protects beliefs but not actions.[4] They apply what is known as the "action-belief" dichotomy as a convenient means in order to determine the scope of the rights protected by the Covenant. This dichotomy, briefly summarised, means that beliefs are accorded absolute protection whereas actions may be subject to regulation. Overlooking the many conceptual problems pertaining to this distinction, the distinction is seductively appealing. Its appeal stems from the fact that the distinction could be used as a convenient guideline to determine what is or what is not protected by the Covenant. Nevertheless, the attractiveness of the distinction may be superficial because the "action-belief" dichotomy overlooks that some actions may be regarded as symbolic speech. Indeed, some actions have been considered by the American Supreme Court as constituting symbolic speech. For example, the wearing of black armbands in breach of an established school policy to denounce the American involvement in the Vietnam war was held to be protected speech, even though the act violated established school policy.[5] In instances of symbolic speech, civil disobedience and freedom of expression overlap conceptually. In an

---

4   Gabriel Moens, "The Action-Belief Dichotomy and Freedom of Religion", 12 *Sydney Law Review*, 1989, 195-217.
5   *Tinker v Des Moines Independent Community School District*, 393 US 503 (1969).

American context, Professor Harrop A Freeman has argued that civil disobedience does come within the protection offered by the First Amendment to the United States Constitution, which incorporates the freedom of expression clause.[6] For support, he refers to *Musser v Utah* where the Supreme Court stated that the "position, that the state may prevent any conduct which induces people to violate the law, or any advocacy of unlawful activity, cannot be squared with the First Amendment."[7]

The importance of the existence of "symbolic speech" for the human rights industry is clear: it forces people to determine which actions are protected by Article 19 of the Covenant. A person's actions may only be justifiable under Article 19 if they rely on, and are inspired by, "higher" principles. I propose to develop some guidelines for the practice of civil disobedience in the next section.

3. Rational civil disobedience

A distinction must be made between the moral and legal justifications for acts of civil disobedience because an act which is morally justified is not necessarily legally justified. The definition of civil disobedience which I introduced in the previous section reveals that a lawbreaker may always seek to justify an act of disobedience by resorting to "higher" moral or religious principles. The morality of an act, however, does not imply its legality. According to a school of thought, acts of disobedience involve the violation of a valid law and, hence, they cannot be justified legally under any circumstances. However, this argument is deficient because some legal systems have provided means by which acts of disobe-

---

6 Harrop A Freeman, "The Right to Protest and Civil Disobedience", 41(2) *Indiana Law Journal*, 1966, 228-254, 242.
7 333 US 95 (1948), 102.

dience can be justified legally following a violation of a valid law. For example, I have already mentioned the effort by the United States Supreme Court to accord constitutional protection to some acts of civil disobedience through its elaboration of the concept of "symbolic speech". Also, other Amendments such as the equal protection and due process clauses have been used by the Court to elevate morally justifiable actions to the status of legally justifiable actions. However, the fact that some acts of disobedience are both morally and legally justifiable does not obviate the need to establish guidelines capable of ascertaining the legality of these acts in most cases.

The legality of an act of civil disobedience depends at least in part, on its rationality. Whilst it is unlikely ever to reach agreement on the rationality of an act because of the ambiguity and vagueness of the concept, its meaning could be clarified by identifying some of its essential features.

First, an act of civil disobedience could be judged by its effectiveness, namely its prospect of success. The effectiveness of an act affects its rationality because an ineffective act is not likely to have any societal impact and, hence, may not result in social change. The requirement that a rational act of disobedience be effective is linked closely to the third essential element in the definition of civil disobedience, namely that acts are undertaken with the purpose of bringing about social change. Acts of direct disobedience which are related directly to the object of protest would, for this reason, be more rational than indirect disobedience because the violated law itself is the object of the protest. Nevertheless, it does not follow that indirect acts of disobedience are irrational simply because they are, arguably, less effective than direct disobedience. For an alleged injustice does not always coincide with specific obnoxious legislation. For example, this is the case when a foreign or domestic policy of the government or an undeclared war is the object of protest. Moreover, a commitment to rationality requires that the higher principles which are invoked by the lawbreaker as justification for an act of disobedience, are balanced against other "higher" principles which require obedience to valid laws. This requirement is important because, otherwise, persons would be encouraged to disobey every law with which they disagree. This would affect undoubtedly the respect for the rule of law and result in instability within a legal system because the very validity of legal rules would be in continuous doubt. This requirement of rationality which requires that "higher" principles be weighed against other, but conflicting, "higher" principles becomes crucial in the light of the fact that acts of disobedience are based often on "higher" principles which are accorded absolute validity by their adherents.

Consider the following example: assume that the law requires compulsory blood transfusion for children whose life is in danger. It is known generally that Jehovah Witnesses object to blood transfusions for religious reasons. Nevertheless, there is a string of cases indicating that Witnesses cannot legally deny blood transfusions for their children. The Witnesses, even though they were practising their religion, were convicted because the interests of the State as *parens patriae* requires that children receive proper medical attention, including blood transfusions, if their life is endangered. These cases, then, are examples of acts of direct disobedience, based on absolute religious principles, which are not weighed against other and equally valid interests.

Thus, people should refrain from breaching a valid law simply because they consider it incompatible with some "higher" principles. In this regard, it is important to remember that one's belief is another's heresy. This has some important implications for a determination of the extent to which an act of disobedience is rational. The desirability of weighing conflicting principles may itself be a compelling reason to delay civil disobedience. A commitment to rationality requires us to determine to what extent a contemplated act of civil disobedience is mixed with self-righteousness and vanity. Therefore, delaying an act of civil disobedience could itself be considered an act of moral courage.

Second, the rationality of an act of disobedience is judged by the willingness of a lawbreaker to accept the penalty imposed for breaching a valid law because it proves their adherence to the system of law whilst, at the same time, expressing his or her disagreement with a specific law. The conscience of society is alerted by the fact that the lawbreaker believes so strongly in their cause because they are willing to go to jail to eradicate the targeted injustices.

Third, the requirement that an act of civil disobedience be rational also requires that the action be commensurate with the alleged injustice which caused a person to disobey the law.

These three requirements would go a long way towards guaranteeing the rationality of an act; they assume that a person who contemplates civil disobedience always tries to avoid unnecessary and needless violations of a valid law. Nevertheless, these requirements are only indications that an act is rational. For example, certain interests could be destroyed effectively through any delaying tactics used by the administration and, in an Australian context, by the requirement that the conformity of a law with the Covenant be tested in a court. "Justice delayed, justice denied" is an important principle of any healthy and mature legal system

4. The lawbreaker as a *ruitenmepper*

Undoubtedly, there are many reasons why civil disobedience takes place. In general, civil disobedience becomes a societal problem when the normal channels of social change do not function properly anymore or whenever serious grievances are not heard. It could be argued that a system does not function adequately anymore when some groups have entrenched power positions in society and use their power to impose their will on weaker or vulnerable classes of people. Indeed, traffic regulations are unlikely to result in disobedience because they affect each member in society equally. But laws that discriminate against classes of people on certain grounds, for example, simply on the ground of race and ethnicity, may well result in civil disobedience. When the opportunities for change which are provided by the legal system are deficient, civil disobedience is often an effective and expeditious way to challenge the law. It is the function of civil disobedience to close the gap that exists between social reality and the law. This process is completed when a lawbreaker can solicit enough support for his or her cause or is able to have their actions considered as "symbolic speech", thereby making them legal.

Civil disobedience, with an avowed intent to challenge a law, is regarded generally as coming within the realm of political activity in democratic countries. However, repeated acts of civil disobedience are an indication that something is wrong in society. The civil disobedient person fulfills the purpose of a *ruitenmepper*, as it is called in the Dutch language: a person who keeps a careful eye on the development of society and who, occasionally, deliberately breaks the law to confront society and its perceived or alleged evils. Civil disobedience, in summary, is strong medicine which renders a society, which otherwise may become less democratic, more responsive to its problems.

3

VALUES CLARIFICATION COURSES IN AUSTRALIAN SCHOOLS: A PARENT'S VIEW
(1989)

1. Human relationship courses

It is a truism that most parents are concerned about the education and welfare of their children. This concern manifests itself in the involvement of parents in the educational process, notably in their membership of, and contributions to, school consultative committees which consider all aspects of the education of children. One of the most contentious aspects of the educational process is the extent to which the contents of the school curriculum should reflect the values and beliefs of parents. Some parents are content to leave all curriculum decisions to professional educators. Others argue that parents have a legitimate expectation to scrutinise the school's curriculum to determine its consistency with traditional values and to expose its hidden agendas, if any.

Queensland's education system has largely reflected, in the past, the values that parents want to inculcate in their children. Parents' concerns about values also dominate the present debate about the desirability of values clarification courses which have been introduced in most States. These courses often have appealing names. For example, in Queensland, they are known as Human Relationships Education (HRE) courses. The Queensland Education Department issued Interim Guidelines for Human Relationships Education in 1988. In these guidelines, a major effort is made to convince parents that the course does not threaten the traditional values of parents and their children. Indeed, it is pointed out that HRE "will be developed and implemented in consultation with parents and the community" and that special emphasis would be placed on the values of "marriage and family life."

Furthermore, one of the principles underlying human relationships education in Queensland State Schools is said to be recognition of parents "as the primary educators in the areas of values and attitudes about family life, roles and behaviours" and that "parents should be closely involved in the development and implementation of HRE programmes in schools to ascertain the specific needs of students and to ensure school-community approval of any program's intentions and practices." However, another principle ominously stipulates that HRE has "implications for the traditional patterns of family relationships that provide security, affection and support" and that the problems and issues within our society should be "acknowledged so that young people understand why people make different life choices."

There is no doubt that most principles upon which HRE is based are laudable. But principles may be subverted by well-meaning professional educators who often have an unquestioned faith in their ability to contribute to the creation of an ideal society. Thus, an assessment of HRE must take into consideration the way in which the relevant principles are implemented by teachers. Specifically, it is necessary to consider whether the introduction of the course has unintended effects which the authors of the principles may not have contemplated. A close analysis of the Guidelines reveals that HRE is merely a sophisticated scheme which makes it possible to attack traditional values cherished by many families. I would like to refer those who question the validity of this statement to another booklet used in an in-service training programme for HRE teachers, entitled *Values Awareness*. This booklet aims to convey one message, namely that there are no absolute values, and that behaviour can neither be described as right or wrong.

This booklet is based on the educational philosophy of Lawrence Kohlberg.[8] In fact, the Kohlberg theory is widely used in HRE courses. He argues that there are six stages in the moral development of people, ranging from primitive hedonism, through conventional morality, to moral judgments based on personal taste and opinion. Most people, according to Kohlberg, do not manage to go beyond the conventional morality stage which requires unquestioned submission to law and order and an allegiance to family and country. But he believes that conventional morality is not good enough and, therefore, he exhorts teachers to raise children to higher stages in moral reasoning. If they successfully pass through this higher stage, children will reach the ultimate objective of "moral autonomy", enabling them to independently decide, without legal restrictions, which laws they will obey. On this view, in matters of sex, drugs and personal behaviour, a child is only liberated if he or she can make an independent decision. It is obvious that this theory denies the existence of moral absolutes

---

8   Lawrence Kohlberg (1927-1987) was an American psychologist. For information on his six stages of moral development, see https://en.wikipedia.org/wiki/Lawrence_Kohlberg%27s_stages_of_moral_development.

and rejects the claim that it is desirable to foster the acceptance by children of "rights" and "wrongs". It is interesting to note that Kohlberg's theory assumes that teachers have already reached that higher level of moral reasoning which is described by the phrase "moral autonomy". But since most teachers would have been exposed to Kohlberg's theories in teacher training colleges and are actively encouraged by various institutions to assume the role of social activists, this should not be totally surprising.

Let me give you some examples of the kind of exercises that children may be expected to participate in when taking a course in HRE. One of the activities is "making a stand". Students are supplied with a list containing controversial activities; they are then asked to indicate on a chart whether they agree or disagree with these activities or whether they are "just part of life". Some of the activities that children are asked to assess are: "having an abortion", "pushing heroin", "having children when not married", and "having sexual relationships before marriage". Before embarking on this so-called educational exercise, children, including those still in primary schools, are told that there are no correct answers and that, therefore, they should not feel constrained by what they have been told or heard at home or in their churches. Such an exercise promotes the fallacious idea that moral autonomy can only be obtained if moral absolutes are replaced by an ad hoc moral philosophy, based on relativism, and dependent on the circumstances of the case. If this activity is done in public, the child who expresses a preference for traditional beliefs may be subject to ridicule for admitting that he or she is no different from their parents and, is, therefore, a long way away from obtaining the Kohlberg goal of "moral autonomy".

Another HRE exercise involves the discussion by students of moral dilemmas. A moral dilemma is described in the Education

Department's booklet as depicting "an issue or situation in which at least two alternative courses of action are available." Again, children are told that there are no right or wrong answers. However, even a perfunctory reading of the examples reveals that there is often a right answer which would command itself to well-thinking citizens. Thus, subject to the validity of my previous points, HRE is nothing else but the imposition upon students of a humanistic, relativistic lifestyle which denies that absolute standards are necessary to maintain a cohesive society, which in turn, is indispensable for the creation of prosperity. Of course, the proponents of HRE, to the extent that they argue that the impartation of absolute moral standards deprives a child from attaining moral autonomy, are themselves guilty of elevating relativism to the status of an absolute principle.

Values clarification courses, in denying the existence of absolute moral values, attack the desire of parents to teach their children traditional Christian values or indeed any form of conventional morality. This philosophy, which now seems to be entrenched in our education system, advocates the implementation of a scheme whereby parents would be excluded from the education of their children altogether. Indoctrination, as we all know, is more likely to be successful when children are impressionable. That is why it is frequently argued by professional educators that attitude changes must be brought about at an early age, in order "to liberate" children from the tribulations of parents' education.

If many discussions with concerned parents are an indication, attitudes instilled in children are often the opposite that parents want. Whereas parents would prefer an emphasis on learning knowledge and skills, professional educators, in pushing these values clarification courses, often tinker with childrens' emotions, attitudes and values. For example, if you would like your children to appreciate that sexual promiscuity is wrong, you should keep them out of Human Relationships courses which are often convenient vehicles to provide children with sex education. Even common sense suggests that children who attend these classes, to a statistically significant extent, become sexually active earlier because they are told safe ways to practice sex without guilt or commitment, with the inference that it is their right to decide on these issues.

Of course, I realise that the negative impact of an HRE course could be cushioned by responsible teachers. If they ae reasonable and intelligent they will use HRE to instil into children, the advantages of traditional Christian values. However, it should not be forgotten that many teachers themselves have at some stage in their training been imbued with the Kohlberg theory. The increased emphasis in professional journals on this theory which sees teachers as "change agents" or "social activists", is reason enough to be diffident about the future.

2. The Human Rights Programme of the Human Rights Commission

It is not unusual for Government publications to describe teachers as "social activists". For example, in an Occasional Paper, entitled *Teaching, enacting and sticking up for human rights* published by the Human Rights and Equal Opportunity Commission,[9] it is stated that the Human Rights Programme, which the Commission promotes in our schools, is "value-heavy ... has explicit ideological commitments, and eschews the notion of

---

9 Colin Henry, David Hitchcock and Michelle Michie, *Teaching, enacting and sticking up for human rights*, Occasional Paper no 9, Australian Government Publishing Service, March 1985.

'neutrality' in education."[10] It is implied that many traditional values are incompatible with the Human Rights Programme or should, at least, be radically altered. Teachers are encouraged by the authors of this paper to become social activists. They also recognise "the need for schools to change if they are to contribute to a new social order that really embodies, rather than pretends to embody authentic democratic principles."[11]

The authors of the Occasional Paper, turning their attention to the Commission's Human Rights Programme for Schools state that the "ultimate intent of the curriculum is emancipatory and reconstructionist: it quite plainly direct teachers to help their students to reflect upon the social, political and economic contradictions in the culture and to take systematic political action against oppressive power blocs."[12] The authors also express the expectation that many teachers will welcome the opportunity to mould the consciences of school children in the interest of social justice.

In this context, it is interesting to mention that the Commission's Human Rights Programme describes Australia as "a liberal, capitalist, multicultural democracy, with social welfare proclivities, a highly stratified class structure, a value system that is secular, racist, sexist and materialistic" and that the institution of "the family reflects and promotes this fact." It is also stated in the Programme that there is "no ideal form of the family." The "construction of a capitalist world economy", so we are told, "is predicated upon dishonesty and greed has slaughtered uncounted millions the world over through the exploitation and the misdevelopment of global resources" and the "United States and the

---

10   Ibid., 72.
11   Ibid., 73.
12   Ibid., 72.

other erstwhile 'free market' democracies have much to answer for in this regard." Those who are interested in the preservation of the present social and political institutions would find these statements in the Commission's Occasional Paper repulsive. My disagreement with these statements stems from the fact that they demonstrate a spectacular inability to distinguish between "indoctrination" and "genuine education". Thus, in the Commission's ideal world, schools would become "social change agents" responsible for changing or, at least modifying the value systems of the children by using the techniques of psychological conditioning.

The Occasional Paper is, of course, not the only educational document that describes teachers as "social activists". For example, not too long ago an American educational journal suggested that the word "teacher" is an anachronism. It favoured the appellation "learning clinician" or "change agent". Schools would become "clinics", the purpose of which would be to provide individualised psycho-social treatment for students! Similarly, Dr Joseph Bean, in several booklets, describes the unceasing and persistent efforts of many American behavioural scientists to denigrate absolute Christian values in the rearing of children. He argues that these scientists lobby for the enactment by Congress of, what they call, "total child development" legislation. In particular, they argue that the "school as a major socialising agency in the community must assume a direct responsibility for the attitude and values of child development" and that the "child advocate, psychologist, social technician and medical technician should ... assume full responsibility for all education, including pre-primary education."

3. The Convention on the Rights of the Child

The rejection, in HRE courses, by many educational policy makers of absolute Christian values is also evident in other developments related to children. As some of you are aware, the Human Rights and Equal Opportunity Commission and UNICEF promote the Convention on the Rights of the Child.[13] They urge the Federal Government to ratify the Convention which is likely to be adopted by the General Assembly of the United Nations in December 1988. Those who favour ratification argue that the implementation of the Convention would substantially reduce the incidence in our society of sexual abuse and emotional deprivation of children. This kind of reasoning could, of course, be easily rebuffed since there is no proven causal relationship between children' abuse and the ratification of the Convention.

A cautious analysis of the Convention reveals that the so-called children' rights entrench the dominance in our society of relativism or situation ethics, which deny the existence of absolute values. For example, Article 13 of the Convention proclaims that, "The child shall have the right to freedom of expression; this right shall include freedom to seek, receive and impart information and ideas of all kinds, regardless of frontiers, either orally, in writing or in print, in the form of art, or through any other media of the child's choice." The child has the right to freedom of expression and the right to seek and to receive information and ideas of all kinds. This Article could easily be interpreted to mean that children, who are defined as persons under 18,[14] have the right to hear and see pornographic materials. Such interpretation would, in any event, be compatible with Article 7 of the revised Humanist

---

[13] This Convention was adopted and opened for signature, ratification and accession by General Assembly resolution 44/25 of 20 November 1989. It became effective on 2 September 1990.

[14] Article 1 of the Convention.

Manifesto II of 1973 which states:

> To enhance freedom and dignity the individual must experience a full range of civil liberties in all societies. This includes freedom of speech and the press, political democracy, the legal right of opposition to governmental policies, fair judicial process, religious liberty, freedom of association, and artistic, scientific, and cultural freedom. It also includes a recognition of an individual's right to die with dignity, euthanasia, and the right to suicide.

Paragraph 1 of Article 14 of the proposed Convention on the Rights of the Child stipulates that the child has the right to freedom of thought conscience and religion. This right is subject only to the parents' right to provide direction and guidance "consistent with the evolving capacities of the child."[15] Thus, if a child rejects parental guidance and direction, it is unlikely that a parent would succeed in inculcating his belief or values in the child. The Convention also provides in Article 15 for the child's right of freedom of association and Article 16 further erodes the rights of parents to supervise the rearing of their children by stating that the child has the right to protection from interference with his privacy or correspondence.

The significance of this Convention lies in the fact that, in substantially eroding the supervisory powers of parents over their children, it promotes the relativistic philosophy which is found in value clarification courses in Australia. In addition, the ratification by Australia of this Convention would extend the power of the Federal Parliament to legislate for children's rights through its external affairs powers. This power could be used to intrude into the sacred domain of the family, leading to more bureaucratic interference with the relationship between parents and children.

---

15 Paragraph 2 of Article 14 of the Convention.

By way of conclusion, I would like to stress that parents should not abandon directive education and should continue to educate their children to enable them to distinguish right from wrong. In this context it is important that we do not equate education and schooling, even though these concepts are often used interchangeably. It is a fallacy to assume that the only education a child obtains takes place in schools. I believe that the home is still a major educational agency despite the high level of family breakdowns. According to statistical evidence each year approximately 50,000 children experience a divorce in the home; thousands of school children now complete their secondary education having experienced two divorces because of the high failure rate of second and subsequent marriages. This high level of family breakdowns adversely affects the education of children. As an increasing number of children do no longer live with their biological parents, the responsibility for education passes to the schools. Indeed, it is fair to say that increasing and incessant pressure is placed on schools to perform many of the educational functions once performed by the family. There may even be problems in families which have not broken down. It is a fact that in many families both parents work out of economic necessity so that no parent can take full-time or near full-time responsibility for the raising of young children. Participation of both parents in the workforce is hardly an educational gain for such children.

There is, of course, a great deal of controversy over whether, and to what extent, the participation of both parents in full-time paid employment adversely affects child development. An enormous amount of result-oriented research in this area is done by people who are ideologically committed and biased, hence I would urge that research findings in this area be carefully examined with healthy scepticism. Also, there is no doubt that a substantial rejection of the "neutrality" of our government schools and a significant weakening of traditional values and morals result in an exodus from state schools. Alternatively, many parents would be forced, because of financial restraints, to send their children to schools that will openly support values and standards that are incompatible with their own.

We should always ask ourselves by what authority schools and teachers take away from parents the responsibility for the general upbringing of their children. It is appropriate, then, that we should reaffirm that parents are and remain the primary educators in the areas of values and attitudes about family life, roles, and behaviour.

4

THE INTERNATIONAL PROTECTION OF MINORITIES:
AN INDIVIDUAL OR GROUP APPROACH?
(1991)

After listening to the informative and entertaining lecture of Mr Asbjorn Eide, I wonder what I could add to the proceedings of this session. Indeed, the speaker discussed, in an exemplary and comprehensive manner, the way in which situations involving minorities could be handled in a peaceful and constructive way. I will nevertheless endeavour to comment briefly on Mr Eide's paper and to offer some points of my own.

In his discussion, Mr Eide identified methods which could be utilised in the future to protect the rights of ethnic minorities. The starting point is Article 27 of the International Covenant on Civil and Political Rights (Covenant):

> In those States in which ethnic, religious or linguistic minorities exist, persons belonging to such minorities shall not be denied the right, in community with the other members of their group, to enjoy their own culture, to profess and practice their own religion or to use their own language.

Article 27, although it appears to be deceptively simple, present us with interpretation challenges. This Article, arguably, does not protect all minorities. The language of the Article indicates that it only covers "ethnic, religious or linguistic minorities" that presently exist within the territory of States. Although the Article makes a distinction between ethnic and linguistic minorities, the two concepts may largely overlap. The issue as to which minorities are protected by Article 27 is further confused because, in the relevant literature, a discussion of the protection of linguistic minorities often figures prominently in the context of an analysis of the concept "ethnicity". Indeed, language is often described as the "most salient symbol of ethnicity because it carries the past and expresses present and future attitudes and aspirations."[16] A commentator on ethnic and linguistic issues, Professor J A S Fishman, wrote in 1976 that, "larger numbers of individuals, in Western as well as in non-Western societies, have recently recognized and even stressed their ethnicity more than was the case just a few years ago"[17] and he suggested that this rebirth of ethnicity is inextricably linked to the increased concerns for the protection of linguistic minorities.

As Article 27 refers to "persons belonging to ... minorities", it protects individuals who belong to minorities, rather than groups. Therefore, only individuals have standing to claim protection

---

16 H Giles, "Introductory Essay" in H Giles (ed.) *Language, Ethnicity and Intergroup Relations*, London, Academic Press, 1977, 4.

17 J A Fishman, "Language and Ethnicity", in H. Giles (ed.) *Language, Ethnicity and Intergroup Relations*, London, Academic Press, 1977, 15.

under the Article. B G Ramcharan confirms that, "Article 27 of the International Covenant on Civil and Political Rights expressly states that it concerns the rights of *persons* belonging to minorities. The drafting history of the article makes it clear that while the rights of persons belonging to minorities are to be enjoyed in community with others, the rights, per se, are primarily individual rights." He adds that, "The doctrine of rights sofar developed by the international community has thus been mainly individualistic."[18]

Is the individual protection of human rights enough to guarantee the rights of minorities? Actions taken by individuals in various jurisdiction certainly suggest that the individual approach is favoured in a world where the persistent and consistent violation of human rights by governments is now recognised as a matter for international concern, resulting in the instigation of judicial measures by individual contestants.

Nevertheless, Article 27 also implies that the rights of persons to practice a religion, and to enjoy their culture and to use their language, are group rights. The Article leaves open the possibility that differential treatment may be needed and positive measures may be introduced in order to enable persons who belong to ethnic minorities to exercise, in community with the other members of their group, the rights granted to them. It is controversial, in international law, whether and if so, to what extent, the rights of groups (as opposed to individuals) can be protected. In this context, it is apposite to refer to paragraph 7 of Article 2 of the United Nations Charter which refers to non-intervention in "matters which are essentially within the domestic jurisdiction of any state...". Article 27 of the Covenant provides for a system of

---

18 B G Ramcharan, "Individual, collective and group rights: History, theory, practice and contemporary evolution", 1(1) *International Journal on Group Rights* 1993, 27-43, 28.

individual protection of the members of an ethnic minority group to guarantee the survival of the group to which these members belong. There is a tension between individual rights, which are enjoyed by persons and the protection of the rights of the group. Indeed, the right of persons to enjoy, in community with others, the rights granted by Article 27, may only be meaningful if facilities are available to enable them to access these rights. But if such facilities were made available, the majority may claim that members of the minority are given differential and preferential treatment.

There are conceptual problems which frustrate any attempts to confer certain rights upon groups. First, there are substantial problems when we attempt to define the concept of an "ethnic minority". I have already referred to the fact that some commentators argue that ethnic minorities largely overlap with linguistic minorities. According to this line of argument, a language is vastly more than a means of communication. It is a powerful symbol of ethnicity. As such, it expresses or evokes several other characteristics which an individual is deemed to possess as a member of an ethnic group. Thus, it is not surprising that one's native language is often assumed to be conclusive evidence of the possession of certain other characteristics which all the members of the language (or ethnic) group are deemed to possess. If language is taken as irrebuttable proof of the existence and possession of other characteristics, then this assumption may well result in the violation of the expectations of some persons who do not want to be included as members of the group.[19] This issue questions our ability to define clearly the nature of an ethnic group and to establish workable guidelines for determining group membership. Indeed, despite a common native language, some persons may not view themselves as members of the group even though they are perceived by oth-

---

19 I deal with this issue in greater detail in Chapter Nine.

ers as members of that group. It is not surprising that discussions about ethnic conflict today are replete with fallacious reasoning because proponents and opponents of the group protection approach too readily assume that a group is a monolithic entity, thereby generating intractable problems with regards to a determination of group membership.

In my experience, many ethnic conflicts are conflicts between group solidarity which is based on a common language, and the rights of persons, either individually or in conjunction with others, to be exempted from membership of the group of which they are deemed to be a member by virtue of a common language. In other words, these conflicts epitomise the tension between the individual and the group approach in the protection of ethnic minorities. It was not always recognised that the individual and the group approach are potentially in tension. For example, the Permanent Court of International Justice in its Advisory Opinion No. 26 of 6 April 1935 on the question of *Minority Schools in Albania* argued that individuals belonging to ethnic minorities should be placed on a footing of perfect equality with the other citizens of the State, and that suitable means must be provided to enable these minorities to preserve their ethnic distinctiveness and traditions. The Court emphasised that these two points were inextricably related and that there "would be no true equality between a majority and a minority if the latter were deprived of its own institutions and were consequently compelled to renounce that which constitutes the very essence of its being a minority."[20]

The above observation is not an exercise in semantics. If we argue that a group is entitled to protection, it becomes necessary to define the concept of an "ethnic minority." At a minimum it would

---

20 Permanent Court of International Justice, Advisory Opinion No. 26 of 6 April 1935 on the question of *Minority Schools in Albania*, para. 52.

be necessary to develop guidelines which enable us to understand the essential features of such groups, and the requirements for group membership. It is, however, not the purpose of my brief comments to define the concept satisfactorily. It suffices for my present purposes to indicate that the task of defining an ethnic minority is usually left to sociologists and anthropologists.

The United Nations, and its constituent committees and commissions, has since its inception also sought to define the concept of an "ethnic minority". Specifically, the Commission on Human Rights has been engaged in the consideration of a Draft Declaration on the Rights of Minorities.[21] Although I assume that not many scholars would question, in principle, the desirability of such a Declaration, they may legitimately express their concerns about its content. If the Declaration were to provide rights in addition to those already granted by Article 27 of the Covenant, the opposition between individual rights and group rights would become greater. This, in turn, may increase the incidence of ethnic conflict, thereby frustrating the very purpose for which the Declaration would be adopted. This concern is legitimate because many draft Articles do not deal with the rights of individuals but with the rights of minority groups. Alternatively, if the United Nations Committee were to defectively paraphrase the existing rights incorporated in Article 27 of the Covenant, then such an approach may have the unfortunate, but largely unintended, consequence that the rights of ethnic minorities are weakened.

---

21 This Draft Declaration was subsequently adopted by the General Assembly resolution 47/135 of 18 December 1992 as the Declaration on the Rights of Persons Belonging to National or Ethnic, Religious and Linguistic Minorities. Paragraph 1 of Article 2 stipulates that, "Persons belonging to national or ethnic, religious and linguistic minorities ... have the right to enjoy their own culture, to profess and practise their own religion, and to use their own language, in private and in public, freely and without interference or any form of discrimination".

The possibility of increased ethnic conflict is real because the proposed Declaration purports to change the nature and the substance of the rights. While Article 27 of the Covenant grants persons belonging to ethnic minorities certain rights to enable them to preserve their cultural identity, the draft Declaration imposes on States the onerous burden of positively promoting the characterisation of the groups concerned. I can only speculate as to why the draft Declaration should embrace such a potentially and, as I will argue, unnecessary course of action which inevitably must lead to increased ethnic tension in societies which have minorities within their borders The manifold, perhaps insurmountable problems, associated with the drafting of a satisfactory Declaration reminds me of the following statement by Tomuschat who said:

> Protection of minorities is not a technical matter which can be successfully accomplished simply by drawing up carefully worded texts. More often than not, relationships between a leading national group and existing minorities are marred by tensions which go far back into the past. Due to a vicious circle of negative mutual experiences, majorities distrust the loyalty of minorities, while minorities resent the intolerant way majorities have oppressed themselves or their ancestors. Almost everywhere in the world a considerable amount of confidence building is required before art 27 can take its full effect.[22]

There are relatively few protection devices which could be used to advance the protection of ethnic minorities. This is not surprising in view of the many conceptual issues associated with the concept of an ethnic minority. Mr Francesco Capotorti who, in the 70s, prepared a United Nations report on the rights of persons belonging to ethnic minorities advocated increased bilateral and regional cooperation, regional seminars, advisory services and fellowships,

---

22 C Tomuschat, "The Protection of Minorities under Article 27 of the International Covenant on Civil and Political Rights", in *Völkerrecht als Rechtsordunung, Internationale Gerichtsbarkeit, Menschenrechte: Festschrift für Hermann Mosler*, 1983, 949.

further studies and education and information activities.[23] It may, however, not be within the scope of human genius to devise lasting solutions aimed at maintaining and protecting minorities which exist within and across borders without fear and hatred being incurred.

I believe that the best way to protect ethnic minorities involves the creation of supranational legal systems, like the legal system of the European Economic Community. This is because the problems faced by ethnic minorities in a State are certainly lessened if that State is subsumed or absorbed by a larger entity which makes national borders obsolete or non-existent. In a larger entity, ethnic minorities become one of many and they may find support from minorities that live across state borders.[24] The idea that ethnic minorities may be effectively protected in a larger entity is, of course, not a new idea. In fact, this idea could be traced back to 1851. In 1851, at the *Congress de la Paix* in Paris, Victor Hugo predicted that, one day, European nations, without losing their characteristics and individuality "will intimately dissolve into a superior entity" and "will constitute the European brotherhood". Hugo's remarkable prophecy was based on the expectation that European battlegrounds would, one day, be transformed into "markets opening to commerce and minds opening to ideas." With this prediction of the dissolution of European nations into a superior entity, Hugo foreshadowed both the creation of the European Community, and the abolition of restrictions on trade, which is one of the stated objectives of the European Community Treaty. My argument is that

---

23 F Capotorti, "Are Minorities Entitled to Collective International Rights?", in Y. Dinstein (ed.) *The Protection of Minorities and Human Rights*, Martinus Nijhoff Publishers, 1952, 505-511.
24 This sentiment expressed in 1991 has proven too optimistic and, possibly, incorrect. Indeed, there have been incessant demands since the 90s for certain ethnic minorities to secede, for example, in Caledonia (Spain) and Scotland (United Kingdom).

the creation of supranational institutions is likely (perhaps, hopefully is a better word?) to overcome the long history of competitive hostility between majorities and minorities that Victor Hugo wrote about so long ago. However, I only express an expectation that tensions will decrease as the consequence of the creation of superrational legal systems. Indeed, the extent to which ethnic minorities will be protected will always depend upon specific government policies pursued by these legal systems.

Finally, it may be argued that the aspirations of ethnic minorities could be met by constitutional arrangements which aim at granting equal partnership status to those groups which have been neglected in the past. At present, there are constitutional developments taking place in Belgium and Spain to harmonise the demands of ethnic groups and the requirements of statehood. These developments aim at bringing about a social order based on some conception of guaranteed political representation within society. For example, these internal arrangements may require equal representation for each ethnic group, including linguistic and other minority groups in society on decision-making forums. Professor Nathan Glazer, in describing several such constitutional arrangements, argues that these arrangements are usually justified on utilitarian grounds, including the claim that they may contribute to a stable political balance and may maintain a democratic and just social order. Specifically, he offers the following insight:

> If we choose the group rights approach we say that the differences between some groups are so great that they cannot achieve satisfaction on the basis of individual rights. We say, too, that ... we will permanently section the society into ethnic groups by law. Even if advocates of group rights claim this is a temporary solution to problems of inequality ... it is inconceivable to me that benefits given in law on the basis of group membership will not strengthen groups, will not make necessary the

policing of their boundaries, and will not become permanent in a democratic society, where benefits once given cannot be withdrawn.[25]

---

25 N Glazer, "Individual Rights Against Group Rights" in E. Kamenka and A. Ehr-Soon Tay (eds.), *Human Rights*, Edward Arnold, 1978, 87-103, 102.

5

HONOURING THE CONTRIBUTIONS OF MOTHERS TO THE FAMILY
A LETTER EXPLORING THE PROPER ROLE OF A CATHOLIC UNIVERSITY
(1991)

I have read with interest the letter written by Professor Kmiec of the University of Notre Dame, South Bend[26] and the reply to it by Mrs Judith Fox, who describes herself as "a faculty wife, a law student, and a mother".[27] For research purposes, I am interested in the way in which prestigious Catholic universities deal with the increasingly difficult problems of upholding and fostering Catholic values in a secular society. Professor Kmiec's letter embedded a resolution, entitled *A Resolution Honoring the Contributions of Mothers*

---

26 *The Observer*, 22 April 1991 (the student newspaper of the University of Notre Dame)
27 *The Observer*, 25 April 1991.

to the Family. It asks the relevant University authorities "to award an additional and significant per child stipend to any married faculty or staff member whose family, in the previous academic year, included a mother who was at home and not employed for compensation with children under 18 years of age."

In my opinion, Mrs Fox's reply contains several sweeping allegations and untruths which seriously distort Professor Kmiec's proposal. Mrs Fox's argument, removed from its supporting considerations, is that, "individuals need to be rewarded for their own accomplishments" and, therefore, male faculty members should not be rewarded solely for their "accuracy in the bedroom." Instead, they should only be rewarded for their own teaching, research, and administrative services which they provide to the University. According to this line of argument, Kmiec's proposal is "insulting to mothers, fathers and human beings in general" because a woman's value or worth would depend upon their ability and willingness to procreate. The proposal, according to Mrs Fox, involves the imposition of Kmiec's ideal of the family upon others, especially those who do not choose to have children. Such imposition violates the rights of people to make their own decisions.

I assume that the above summary is a reasonably good restatement of Mrs Fox's argument. Her argument could be criticised for its use of emotional language, which unnecessarily deflects from the rigour (or lack of it) of her reasoning. Mrs Fox, in her letter, certainly weakens her case by constantly using overinclusive language, for example, by claiming that the Kmiec proposal is insulting to *all* women and human beings. The attribution of Mrs Fox's point of view to *all* people constitutes an imposition on those who disagree with her statements.

Nobody would disagree, at least not in public, with the proposition that people should be paid for their own accomplishments and the value of their services to the University. There is nothing in Kmiec's proposal that would indicate his disagreement with this proposition. If so, his proposal has been misinterpreted by Mrs Fox. In what way? Mrs Fox, in her reply, fails to make a distinction between the essence of Professor Kmiec's proposal and the means to achieve the proposal's objectives. Even if the means are considered inappropriate, unpractical, or unrealistic, the essence of the proposal might still be valuable and survive the scrutiny of the members of our Catholic university community.

Professor Kmiec's proposal is that, in the Year of Women, a Catholic University should meaningfully honour mothers, who unselfishly devote their time to the raising and the nurturing of their children. Such honour and recognition is in accordance with the encyclical teaching of the Catholic Church as espoused by Pope John Paul II who has stated that, "society must be structured in such a way that wives and mothers are not in practice compelled to work outside the home, and that their families can live and prosper in a dignified way even when they themselves devote their full time to their own family."[28] According to Professor Kmiec, mothers could be honoured suitably by awarding an additional per child allowance to those faculty and staff members whose families includes a full-time mother at home with children under 18 years of age.

My point is that reasonable people may agree with Professor Kmiec's proposal in principle yet disagree with his preferred method of implementation. Mrs Fox's rejection of the essence of the Kmiec proposal is problematic because, in claiming that faculty members would be paid not for their skill in the classroom but for the number of their children, she exclusively focusses on the

---

28 *Familiaris Consortio*, 22 November 1981.

method by which mothers may be honoured. From an intellectual point of view, it is wrong to condemn the proposal as reprehensible and insulting simply because one disagrees with the means to achieve the proposal's objectives. The use of emotive language is not a substitute for cogent reasoning.

The proposal to honour mothers is commendable because, using the language of Pope John Paul II, "the mentality which honors women more for their work outside the home than for their work within the family must be overcome" and that this entails "that men should truly esteem and love women with total respect for their personal dignity, and that society should create and develop conditions favoring work in the home."[29] In this context, it is also appropriate to remind the readers of this letter that the Catholic Church has always stressed the importance of the family wage and has advocated the payment of family allowances or grants to mothers who devote themselves exclusively to their families.

However, even if I am compelled to argue on Mrs Fox's plane, Kmiec's proposal would still survive critical scrutiny precisely for the reasons used by Mrs Fox to reject the proposal as insulting. Mrs Fox's argument, as observed above, is that faculty or staff members should be paid for their own accomplishments and the quality of the performance of their teaching, research, and administrative duties. I agree. But I disagree with her conclusion that the Kmiec proposal is incompatible with her argument. Why? Most of us know (though not all of us will have the courage to admit it) that, in general, faculty members with supportive wives (who may also be mothers), become more productive academics than those who may not be in a position to devote all their time to their University duties. Marital problems and unsupportive wives and mothers inevitably and adversely affect the quality of an academic's

---

[29] *Familiaris Consortio*, 22 November 1981.

work. Usually, the value of an academic's work to the University increases as a direct consequence of the staff member's ability to concentrate on his University duties. This increased value, in turn, is due at least in part, to the existence of a supportive wife and mother. The conclusion which could reasonably be drawn is that an additional allowance for married staff members whose families include a mother would accurately reflect the increased worth of the academic to the University.

This argument may not be palatable to all readers. They may even chastise the author of this letter for his inability to come up with supporting statistical or empirical evidence to support his claim that a supportive wife and mother favourably influences the quality of an academic's work. However, my reasoning involves the development of an argument that appeals to common sense. In any event, considering the sensitivity of this issue, it would be difficult to collect the necessary statistical evidence to convince my critics of the plausibility of my argument. In summary: subject to the validity of my argument, an academic with a full-time wife and mother at home himself deserves a substantial salary increase to compensate him for the additional energy and competence which he may bring to his University work. This, in turn, also indirectly compensates the academic's wife for she knows that her efforts in maintaining a happy family home and nurturing of children leads to, or results in, greater family prosperity. This conclusion is eminently reasonable, especially in times when tax policies increasingly burden the single-income family.

I do not find the Kmiec proposal insulting. In fact, his proposal has been carefully drafted. His proposal does not discriminate between male and female faculty staff members. Indeed, according to his proposal, the per child allowance would be available even if a full-time father devotes his life to the raising of his children. In an important footnote, the existence of which was conveniently overlooked by Mrs Fox, Professor Kmiec specifically states that it is "logical and meritorious for the university to extend the benefits of this resolution ... to include married faculty or staff families with a father at home under parallel circumstances." Thus, the proposal does not affect the way in which husband and wife may wish to divide their work. The proposal is pro-choice.

It may be argued, however, that the proposal is defective to the extent that it seeks to exclude from the proposed payment of additional allowances, those female faculty members who are also devoted mothers and wives. Also, the proposal does not provide for compensation if a male faculty member has a childless wife at home. These comments, however, relate to the means that could be used to implement the Kmiec proposal. Refinements to the proposal could easily have been made following extensive deliberations of the Faculty Senate. It is deplorable that the Faculty Senate declined to discuss, for want of a seconder, Professor Kmiec's Resolution Honoring the Contribution of Mothers to the Family. In failing to discuss his proposal, the Faculty Senate has denied itself the opportunity to discuss the proper role of a Catholic University in this context. The Senate's decision is surprising because a prestigious University is presumably dedicated to the concept of academic freedom and the relentless pursuit of truth. The failure of the Faculty Senate to proceed to a discussion of the Kmiec proposal also sits uncomfortably with the encyclical teaching of the Catholic Church. Do I assume that the Church's pronouncements are irrelevant in a Catholic University which is trying to survive in an ocean of secularism? But, as Hugo Adam Bedau said, "this is the right place to end the present investigation because we have reached the launching platform for another one."

6

SPEECH TO CELEBRATE THE NATIONAL CIVIL COUNCIL 50TH ANNIVERSARY

(1991)

A few weeks ago, I was asked by Mr Brian Mullins[30] to speak at the 50th Anniversary Celebration of the Movement. Specifically, he suggested that I might comment upon the history of the Movement and the leadership it has provided in Australia for five decades. I explained to Mr Mullins that I was not suitably qualified to perform this function. I reminded him of the fact that I arrived in Australia on 1 January 1975 and, therefore, I was largely unfamiliar with the work of the Movement and its contributions to the religious and political events of the 50s and 60s. Even if I had been in Australia at that time, I would have been too young to realise and to appreciate the importance of the Movement's work. Nevertheless, I willingly succumbed to the admirable tenacity and

---

30 Brian Mullins (1925-2009) was President of the National Civic Council (NCC) in Queensland from 1960 to 2000.

persuasion of the State President. I am delighted to take part in tonight's celebration, to highlight the Movement's considerable contribution to Australia and to honour the Movement's undisputed Leader, Mr Bartholomew Augustine (Bob) Santamaria.

The birth and the history of the Movement is documented in Mr Santamaria's autobiography, entitled *Against the Tide*.[31] In preparation for tonight's address, I reread this book which describes much of Australia's post Second World War history. It appears to me that the fifty-year history of the Movement can be divided into three distinct periods. The first begins with the formation in 1941 of the Movement and ends with the great Australian Labor Party (ALP) Split in the mid-50s. Most members of the Movement were Catholic ALP sympathisers, who were justifiably abhorred by the increasing, and initially, successful attempts by the Communist Party of Australia (CPA) to grab political power by organising several debilitating industrial strikes. During that period, the Movement was certainly the most important organisation which struggled against Communist infiltration in Australian unions. A Melbourne academic, Dr Manne recently stated that the CPA "was a fully totalitarian political organization, dominated both organisationally and ideologically by Stalin's Soviet Union; a party which injected into the political culture of early post-war Australia the alien mentality and methods of one of the most sinister regimes in the history of mankind."[32] Mr Santamaria recognised the totalitarian nature of the CPA and decided to counter its influence by establishing Industrial Groups in key unions. This struggle was carried on initially with the support of the Catholic Hierarchy, especially the legendary Archbishop

---

31 Bartholomew Augustine Santamaria, *Against the Tide*, Oxford University Press, Bowen Crescent, Melbourne, 1981.
32 Robert Manne, "The Fiftieth Anniversary of the National Civic Council", *News Weekly*, 26 October 1991, 11.

of Melbourne, Dr David Mannix. The achievements of the Movement were spectacular. By the end of 1953, most unions were returned to non-communist control. Not unexpectedly, however, the achievements of the Movement were reviled by its enemies. These enemies accused the Movement of zealotry, a penchant for secrecy and a willingness to utilise means which were disproportionate to the alleged dangers posed by Communism. The accomplishment of the Movement and of its Industrial Groups were denigrated by their opponents who claimed, among other things, that the Communist threat to democratic institutions was highly exaggerated. The unpleasantness associated with the denigration of the Movement was, however, only a prelude to the momentous Labor Split of the mid 50s, which was also when the second period in the history of the Movement began.

In October 1954, the then Leader of the Opposition, Dr Evatt, launched a vicious attack on the Industrial Groups which had been established in the unions. His fateful decision to destroy the Movement was probably a direct consequence of Dr Evatt's narrow electoral defeat in May 1954. In attacking the Movement, Dr Evatt attempted to maintain the leadership of the ALP by appeasing the Left. His attack, followed by the subsequent Labor Split, resulted in the creation, by union organisers, of the Democratic Labor Party (DLP). It also provided the CPA with renewed opportunities to foment social unrest. As the CPA's activities were no longer directly opposed by the ALP, Communist attempts to infiltrate the union movement were increasingly successful. It is common knowledge that for eighteen years, until 1972, the Split was responsible for keeping the ALP in opposition. This strategy was known within the Movement at the time as the "Roadblock". It could be argued that the failure to withdraw support for its pro-communist left wing, and the maintenance of unity tickets with communists whilst avoiding rapprochement with the anti-communist working class Catholics of the DLP, resulted in the ALP being in opposition for such a long time.

During these momentous events of the 50s, many Catholic Bishops, who had enthusiastically supported the Movement before the Labor Split, effectively changed sides, and sought to control the Movement. Perhaps, the Bishops may have been motivated by pragmatism and a sincere desire to maintain industrial peace. Nevertheless, their change of heart must have insulted Mr Santamaria, who in his exemplary life always tried to give practical expression to Catholic principles. Mr Santamaria's support for the Catholic Church is well-known and is exemplified in the principal authorship of most of the Bishops' Social Justice statements, published between 1941 and 1956. We all expect to be betrayed by our enemies, but we do not expect our friends to become disloyal. Mr Santamaria, despite the power struggle for control of the Movement, continued to remind the Australian public of the dangers of Communism and the incompatibility of that ideology with the social principles of the Catholic Church. He had the courage to stand by his principles, even when he was abandoned by much of the Catholic Hierarchy. Under these circumstances, it is no wonder that it became necessary to transform the Movement into an organisation, known as the National Civic Council (NCC), which no longer had a direct relationship with the Catholic Church. This outcome, however, may have had the effect of galvanising the efforts of Catholic and non-Catholic people into an effective anti-communist force. But there have been moments of difference and, indeed, tension between the Bishops and the NCC since the creation of the Council

The Movement entered its third phase with the election of the Whitlam Government in 1972. The assumption of power by the ALP obviously defeated the Roadblock strategy and resulted in the demise of the DLP as a political power. Although in the 70s and 80s, the fight against Communism continued, the National Civic Council and its publication, News Weekly, increasingly concentrated on the dangers of, what could conveniently be referred to as, "the philosophy of relativism and humanism". According to this philosophy, it is inappropriate to judge the morality of a person's behaviour, provided it does not harm other people. This philosophy involves "the belief that all approaches to truth are relative to particular situations".[33] In particular, the Movement and its leaders courageously and consistently alerted Australians to the existence of the fallacious assumption upon which many pieces of social engineering legislation are based. The Movement provided a much-needed alternative point of view on such issues as abortion, affirmative action for women and disadvantaged groups in society, the role of the homemaker, marital fidelity, euthanasia, and biogenetics. It encouraged Australians, especially young people, to appreciate the role of traditional social, religious, and moral values in the maintenance of the social fabric

Now that the shackles of Communism are effectively discarded and the moral bankruptcy of this ideology is revealed, the Left aggressively imposes a social agenda in which it seeks to mandate conformity with its relativistic and humanistic values across the range of human behaviour. Thus, we find that traditional human behaviour is vilified as a vituperative expression of sexism or racism. Encouragement for the vocation of homemaker is described as a particularly odious form of sexism. Instead, feminism, preferential treatment, alternative lifestyles, infidelity, and politically correct speech, just to name a few, are variously described as desirable or even liberating orthodoxies. These new orthodoxies, which are often aggressively promoted by well-funded lobby groups, create a

---

33 G Pell, "N.C.C. 50th Anniversary Celebration – Bishop Pell's Address", *AD 2000 – A Journal of Religious Opinion*, vol.4(10), November 1991, 13.

climate of intolerance, and instil a sense of genuine fear into a great number of decent people. Interestingly, the similarities between Communism and the present orthodoxies are more striking than their dissimilarities. By this I mean that both Communism and many of the so-called "progressive" ideas in our society assume that Man can fashion the ideal world. Those who are deemed to be enlightened enough to see the value of these new orthodoxies then proceed to impose them upon the other members of society. Thus, it is necessary to point out that relativism and humanism are nothing else but sophisticated manifestations, like Communism until its spectacular collapse, of an obsession to create the "ideal" World which is totally divorced from God.

As I understand it, the fight against relativism and humanism and the defence of traditional values is a high priority of the National Civic Council. The Council is ideally placed to equip people with the philosophic knowledge and confidence needed to erode the specious arguments of the relativists and humanists and their brave New World ideas. I can well imagine that the sympathisers of the NCC feel like David who fights against a powerful Goliath. Those who dare to stand up for decency are described as "barbarians" or "dinosaurs" who oppose inevitable progress. There is no doubt that the defence of traditional values is a most difficult task. This difficulty stems from the fact that leftist reformers often do not directly reject conventional concepts but seek to accommodate with them some new project that may be substantially inconsistent with the conventional understanding of the concept. Friedrich von Hayek, commenting upon this difficulty states that, "one must today hesitate to use even words like 'liberty', 'justice', 'democracy' or 'law', because they no longer convey the meaning they once did"[34] His point is that the decay or corruption of language has

---

34 Friedrich Hayek, *The Political Order of a Free People*, Routledge & Kegan Paul, London, 1979, 135.

helped to seduce people to serve what they imagined to be good purposes. Perhaps, Hayek's point explains why many people fail to live in accordance with what they instinctively know to be right. Furthermore, the problems associated with the defence of traditional values are exacerbated by the constant exposure of people to television programmes that unashamedly embrace the agenda of the leftist agitators and reformers. I have heard it said that television is the worst invention of the 20th century! Although I question the validity of this sentiment, there is little doubt that there are opportunistic people who use modern inventions, including television, for their corrupting purposes.

It is not my function tonight to assess comprehensively the impact of the new orthodoxy on our rights. For my present purposes, it suffices to express my belief that the new orthodoxy progressively erodes our ability to freely express our opinions. There are many pieces of legislation which, collectively, amount to an impressive and sustained assault on freedom of expression. These pieces of legislation, if assessed individually, sound deceptively reasonable and innocent. But their collective impact upon freedom of expression is profound. Other pieces of legislation increase the extent to which people become dependent on the Government, thereby relieving individuals from the responsibility to look after their own welfare. It creates an all-powerful Government and an impotent, submissive, and obedient group of citizens. With Henry David Thoreau, I tend to believe that, in an ideal world, the best government is a government that governs least[35] but creates a climate in which it is possible for people to better themselves. Incidentally, today is United Nations Human Rights Day. Today, we are acutely aware of the necessary link between freedom of expression and the preservation of a healthy democracy. Many

---

35 Henry David Thoreau, *Resistance to Civil Government*, para. 1.

people who are fortunate enough to live in democratic societies take freedom of expression for granted and do not realise that the price for freedom is eternal vigilance.

A great Australian who, for five decades now, has assiduously worked for the preservation of that basic freedom in our society is the Leader of the National Civic Council, Mr Bob Santamaria. Mr Santamaria has given Australia leadership, vision, and strength. It is certain that the enemies of the NCC do not want to be reminded of the invaluable work that Mr Santamaria has done and continues to perform. But we will not forget. We will not forget that, due to this effort, Australians live in a country that is free from the worst excesses of totalitarianism and arbitrary oppression. But the fight for freedom, and therefore the work of the NCC, inevitably remains unfinished business.

We have assembled today to celebrate the 50th Anniversary of the Movement and the Leadership provided by Mr Santamaria for five decades. I have had an opportunity to listen to Mr Santamaria on several occasions. I am impressed by the Cartesian clarity of his analysis of national and international affairs. The clarity and coherence of his ideas are matched by his sincerity, genuineness, and modesty. He has an unusual ability to identify the issues that matter most and to bring his considerable personal, intellectual, and practical knowledge to bear on them. His strength lies in the fact that he can perceive their significance and likely impact upon the cohesiveness of our society.

Mr Santamaria could easily have achieved high political office if he had been willing to make opportunistic compromises, for which many of our politicians are so rightly reviled. Instead, he chose to sacrifice a profitable career for the pursuit of higher ideals. He has made this country a better place to live in. Our gratitude, even if expressed profusely, is but a poor substitute for the praise which Mr Santamaria so richly deserves. I express the hope that the work of the National Civic Council and its Leader, Mr Santamaria, will continue and flourish for a long, long time.

7

AN ASSESSMENT OF AUSTRALIAN EDUCATION
(1992)

On 28 November 1991, the Deans of the Faculties of Arts in Australian Universities issued a press release in which they commented upon the demonstrable inability of many Australian university students to express themselves properly orally and in writing. This deplorable situation, if true, can only be attributed to the fact that increasing numbers of students do not enjoy a sound high school education which prepares them for the challenges, and opportunities, of university studies.

The proportion of students now continuing to the end of high school has risen to over 50% of the total high school student body. This is a significant statistic since, thirty years ago, only the best students, the top four or five percent, succeeded to finish high school and enter universities. Not only are students encouraged to stay in school, but it is also government policy that as many students as possible obtain a university education. Professor David Myers, the Convenor of the Deans of the Faculties of Arts, commenting upon these developments, revealed that universities "now admit students who would never have got near a university even ten years ago."

Those of us who have or had children in high schools and are seriously concerned about the quality of Australian education could not have failed to notice the alarming signs which are symptomatic of decline. Although teaching of language skills, including grammar, punctuation and spelling has always been a mandatory requirement in primary and secondary English syllabuses in Queensland, many students cannot properly spell. This is probably a consequence of the remarkably dominant position of Systemic-Functional Grammar in the field of English language education in Australia. As I understand it, Systemic-Functional Grammar, which is derived primarily from the work of Professor M A K Halliday of Sydney, does not require mastery of the traditional rules of grammar and is based on the assumption that the study of these rules inhibits a student's spontaneity. In response to a request for information, a Senior Policy Officer of the Department of Education confirmed that the "grammar advocated by the department derives essentially from systemic function linguistics and therefore is a grammar of English (and not Latin) that deals with meaning as well as structure." The downgrading of the teaching of the rules of grammar is supported by many educational policymakers, including some academics. For example, Professor John Frow, Professor of English at the University of Queensland, condemned in his inaugural lecture the "rigidly normative teaching of language skills" and quoted, with approval, Colin MacCabe's attack on those with an obsessive need to avoid split infinitives and are meticulous in distinguishing "will" and "shall".

Some students finish high school without being able to distinguish between an adjective and an adverb. Many people, including some who consider themselves to be educated, do not realise that their linguistic abilities are deficient. Even a perfunctory reading of newspaper articles reveals that they are replete with many grammatical errors. For example, we regularly hear statements which contain a subject noun in the plural, yet the verb remains in the singular as when a person says: "the problems is serious", or "is there any questions?" Another example is provided by the tendency to use the pronoun "they" instead" of "he" or "she" when referring to a single person.

The failure to ensure the grammatical correctness of one's use of language is an endemic problem in Australia. When I was writing this paper, one of my students provided me with her assessment of the problem. It is worthwhile to quote her deposition in full:

> Based on my own high-school and university experience, very little, if any grammar is taught in high schools today. At high school I was a top student in English and French. This was mostly as a result of my parents' teaching me grammar and grammatical rules at home. When a native French teacher arrived to teach French in my senior year, she was appalled at the standard of grammar in our class. The students, with two notable exceptions, could not give an example of a conditional or subjunctive verb in English. Nor could many give an example of the imperative in English. Thus, the French teacher took on the duty for one month (or more) of teaching her year 12 French students basic English grammar. Even at the end of Grade 12, many could not explain or give examples of those verb tenses.
>
> This "modern" learning by usage method does not work for English language teaching in Australian high schools. I was taught more new words in Grade 6 and 7 than in Grades 8, 9 and possibly 10. There is no revision or memorisation of grammar or vocabulary. Few, if any students could competently state which

was the subject, adverb, noun, etc., in a sentence.

I am not referring to a government-funded school with overcrowded classes, but rather an exclusive Brisbane private girls' school with reasonably sized classes.

Fortunately, my parents were taught under the old system.

Our high-school students are not exposed to enough learning. High-school students usually spend fewer days or hours in school than in other industrialised countries. This problem is exacerbated when valuable school time is lost for the pursuit of activities which are not likely to increase the intellectual powers of students. I refer to swimming or athletics competitions, which must be compulsorily attended by all students, visits to television stations and community organisations, camps and even the running of religious services during school time.

If my experience is an indication, many teachers abandon their teaching duties by playing videotapes, which are only indirectly or remotely related to the studies of the students. Typically, these teachers attempt to justify their constant use of videotapes on the ground that it is necessary to diversify the learning experiences of students; in fact, it is often a convenient tool to hide their lack of enthusiasm and incompetence

There is a failure, in some schools, to reward academic excellence. Too much emphasis is being placed on sporting and extra-curricular activities to the point where being bright at school almost certainly leads to unpopularity. Those who win prizes in athletics, tennis, swimming, are praised and rewarded in front of the whole school, and in the school's newsletters. Their names are proudly engraved on trophies which are displayed in the school's trophy cabinet. But those who achieve a comparable level of excellence in their schoolwork are virtually ignored by the school community –

in some cases even by the teachers. I am not saying that we should not encourage and reward our sporting heroes at school. But I mean that, when glorifying students, we should strike a healthy balance between those who achieve academically and those who achieve in extra-curricular activities, including sporting events. While there are bright students who will still achieve academic excellence, despite this lack of recognition, there are borderline students who may be encouraged to study harder if they know their reward will be more than just personal satisfaction. There are simple ways to promote academic excellence in a school, including:

- the encouragement to read about and to research further the topics discussed in class, with higher marks given to those who demonstrate a willingness to undertake further work,
- the establishment of academic prizes each year or semester for each subject,
- the organisation of a speech night for junior and senior levels,
- the running of academic competitions, such as essay and poetry writing competitions,
- the selection of a dux of the class or school.

The educational philosophy which requires the discouragement of high achievers is aggressively promoted by many teachers in this country. Those who dare to question the desirability or propriety of implementing this philosophy are usually regarded as reactionaries who are out of touch with some modern, yet largely untested, education teaching theories. Conversely, students who, by any standard, fail to excel, might be rewarded with high marks and encouragement which convey to them the illusion of achievement. How is it possible to inculcate in students the values of excellence, achievement, and pride if these values are treated with hostility by increasing numbers of teachers, who often are only interested in imposing upon students their preferred ideological and philosophical rhetoric?

This assessment of Australian high school education is not, of course, the result of a comprehensive sociological survey but is based on my experience as a university lecturer, and knowledge of the education system. To discredit my assessment, educational bureaucrats may refer to a report entitled *Assessment of Student Performance 1990* published in 1991. The summary on page 114 of that report indicates that 90% of students in Year 9 in government and non-government schools consistently and correctly control key language features such as cohesion, grammar, paragraphing, vocabulary, punctuation, and spelling when writing. But even common sense would suggest that the validity of this assessment by the education authorities depends on the difficulty of the administered tests and the students' expected level of achievement.

I do not claim that these problems exist in every school or to the same extent. But I believe that these problems are not completely absent from any school. This belief stems from the fact that, in my opinion, a climate of mediocrity is nurtured in our high schools, which increasingly are no longer exclusively used for educational purposes. Instead, they function as convenient custodians of those who, otherwise would wreak havoc on society and would make demands on the welfare state. The claim that high schools are increasingly used for custodial, as opposed to purely educational purposes, is not preposterous. My colleague, Associate Professor Philip de Lacey of the University of Wollongong recently argued that the increased retention rate means that teachers of the last two years of high school are no longer able to maintain previous standards, their classes being filled, and often disrupted, by senior pupils who are attending for custodial rather than educational reasons. His point was reinforced recently by a report in the *Courier-Mail* of 26 March 1992 on the increasing violence in the playground of schools. According to the report, teachers at Beenleigh High School are afraid to do playground duty because of increasing violence among students. The article reported that teachers were threatened, and girls had been raped. In addition, there were other school-related assaults when gangs of youths from various schools gathered at train stations and attacked each other. The relevance of these events to critics of the education system is that government policies aimed at increasing the high school retention rate, are based on the fallacious assumption that all students who stay on at high school will necessarily benefit from their involvement with their schools.

It is necessary to consider the consequences of (a) using high schools as custodial rather than educational institutions, and (b) the relentless pressure upon students to seek a university education. The Deans of the Faculties of Arts in Australian universities reported that many students are unable to understand the standard set texts and cannot express anything but the simplest thought in clear prose. The press release of 28 November 1991 refers to the results of a test, administered by a senior academic. The test revealed that the best student could define the meaning of only five words out of 12 chosen from one paragraph in a set reference text. One student, whose first language was English, could define only one word. These words were: imperative, kindred, concurred, indelibly, annals, exterminating, aggravating, corroboration, commiseration, indictment, ordinance, deplore. Because of the deteriorating standards in high schools, many lecturers in University Arts departments teach basic communication skills, since it can no longer be assumed that students possess these skills. In this context, it is perhaps appropriate to quote once more from the deposition of my student, to which I have already referred:

In advanced French classes at the University of Queensland, the lecturers were teaching the equivalent of Grade 9 and 10 French in some cases. After two years of French we still had not tackled the rules for the subjunctive and conditional. Only mature age students could understand the different tenses in English.

A Dean of Arts, who attended the Conference of Deans on 28 November 1991 said that, "sporadic testing has demonstrated beyond reasonable doubt that a greater percentage of first year students in History at the University of Wollongong do not understand much of what they hear in lectures and tutorials, and what they are asked to read." Consequently, an increasing number of University lecturers revert or regress to being teachers of junior secondary English. Others simply lower their standards to accommodate the invasion of under-achievers; some lecturers are under not so subtle pressure to lower their standards. It is a sign of the times that the Department of Classics at the Australian National University now offers a course in basic grammar, not only for Classics students but for all comers. There is also evidence, some of which is described in my book *The Decline of the University*,[36] that, in some departments, students with a poor high school education become aggressive when scholarly, sophisticated language is used by their lecturers.

There is no doubt that extra resources would be needed to provide remedial training to students who are victims of our present high school education system. However, it is unlikely that these resources will be made available in times of recession and monetary restraint. Professor David Myers points to the need for further funds in the press release of 28 November 1991. He laconically states that if "the Government is to maintain its present policies in increasing access to university education, it must do all it can to see that the universities develop non-traditional methods for

---

36 Philip de Lacey and Gabriël Moens, *The Decline of the University*, Law Press, 1990.

teaching non-traditional students" and "that will mean increased funding for experiment and equipment". His statement seems to suggest that Universities should be in the business of providing high school education to non-traditional students if tertiary institutions are provided with funds for this purpose. Although I understand the logic of Professor Meyers' argument, it nevertheless conflicts with the function of the University which, as defined by Alfred North Whitehead, is the imaginative impartation and extension of knowledge:

> The justification for a university is that it preserves the connection between knowledge and the zest of life, by uniting the young and the old in the imaginative consideration of learning. The university imparts information, but it imparts it imaginatively. At least, this is the function which it should perform for society. A university which fails in this respect has no reason for existence.[37]

Indeed, it could hardly be argued that it is the function of universities to graduate increasing numbers of people who, whilst they are surrounded by books, are unable to distinguish between what is and what is not worth reading.

The problems generated by the use of universities for the purpose of offering remedial education are likely to be exacerbated if the Commonwealth, as expected, moves to "output funding" (or payment by results) which makes payments to universities dependent upon the number of students actually graduating. If such a proposal were adopted, there would be relentless pressures upon universities to dilute further existing standards of scholarship, academic excellence, and objectivity. A system of payments by results would certainly result in an increase in the

---

[37] A N Whitehead, *The Aims of Education and Other Essays*, Ernest Benn Ltd, London, 1962, 138-139.

number of Australia's graduates. But it is preposterous to suggest that such process would result in Australia becoming a "clever" country. In fact, it would result in encouraging and perpetuating mediocrity.

In Australia, as already indicated, the retention rate in high schools has increased from below 20% to 50% in less than 25 years. This means that universities now take in the failures they used to reject. Many of our students, especially those studying at former colleges of advanced education, lack the cultural and intellectual background that university academics assumed their students had. One Dean of Arts is reported as having said that many non-traditional students simply "cannot bring to bear on the study of social and cultural problems the body of information that we had when we were in their place." He went on to say that their command of the English language, speaking, reading, and writing is not at the level of competence we used to assume. The reading of the great writers of Western civilisation is now seen as an imposition and as culturally discriminatory. Indeed, a dislike for the great writers, coupled with incessant demands to use non-sexist language, which is imposed rather than spontaneously developed, leads to the further demand to reconstitute the compulsory reading list in university Arts faculties. Such a demand was made successfully at Stanford University, where feminists succeeded in substituting non-sexist and non-racist books for the traditional classics of the world's literature.

A government policy which pretends that young people enjoy a university education when they are exposed to remedial high school teaching, is wrong for moral as well as economic reasons. It is wrong from a moral point of view because it deprives students of a genuine university education while pretending that remedial education is the real thing; it is wrong from an economic point of view because it involves the spending of large sums of money on people who may not be able to profit from, and to contribute to, a university education. Nevertheless, present educational policymakers insist that as many students as possible should be encouraged to attend university, even if it means the transformation of universities into glorified high schools which redirect part of their scarce resources to remedial teaching. Specifically, these policymakers argue that the admission of these students who often come from disadvantaged social and ethnic backgrounds, is beneficial because it results in a diverse student body. On this line of argument, a diverse university student population has, from an educational point of view, a salutary effect upon students because the interaction between members of different social and ethnic groups results in a greater understanding of the world around us.

This argument is certainly not novel and is, in fact, being aggressively and assiduously pursued overseas, especially in the United States. For example, Dinesh D'Souza effectively succeeds in demystifying the diversity argument in his best-selling book *Illiberal Education: The Politics of Race and Sex on Campus*.[38] His book illustrates that, to some significant extent, a person's rights depend upon group membership and that criticism of the diversity policy is likely to be viewed as an abuse of one's right to freedom of speech. His book is also a timely reminder of the fact that this diversity or group rights' approach remains largely incompatible with the traditional emphasis on individual rights

My point is that, in Australia, the present concern to increase the student bodies on campuses is yet another example of the implementation of the diversity philosophy. The diversity philosophy (or principle) is also often applied to the recruitment

---

38 Dinesh D'Souza, *Illiberal Education. The Politics of Race and Sex on Campus*, The Free Press, New York, 1991.

of university staff. In such cases, the principle is sought to be implemented by the adoption of equal opportunity employment programmes. For example, in its meeting of 15 October 1990, the Senate of the University of Queensland approved in principle a policy for gender equity in committee representation. This policy requires or provides for the inclusion of a 25% minimum representation of the minority gender, greater flexibility in eligibility for committee membership, co-option of external representatives to achieve the 25% minimum and promotion of the policy among pro vice-chancellors, deans and heads of departments. This decision, which in effect provides for a quota, weakens the University's claim that it exclusively deals with people based on individual merit.

This decision is merely an example of a general trend in Australian universities to bring about a more diverse committee structure. In my opinion, treatment based on individual merit requires that applicants be selected and promoted on the basis of their ability to contribute to, and to profit from, their involvement with the function of the university. In general, university academics themselves are to be blamed for what happens in universities in the name of "equal opportunity". The Federated Australian University Staff Association, FAUSA, in 1990, insisted, during discussions with University employers that there should be a 50% gender balance across all levels of university employment. Although the union representatives explained that this was an ambit claim, and therefore a deliberate exaggeration, it will not be remembered as the Association's most valuable contribution to the ideals that universities should be seen to protect.

The thrust of my argument is that high schools and universities are more and more used for purposes which are extraneous to their functions The provision of remedial teaching by tertiary institutions in order to enable the implementation of the diversity principle is an apt, but not an isolated, example of this trend.

In recent years, students and academics have endured quite dramatic changes to universities and colleges of advanced education. These changes have been justified by their proponents on utilitarian and social justice grounds. We have seen the relentless pursuit by governments of economies of scale, most visibly manifested in the wave of institutional amalgamations. Governments, as I have argued, have also imposed heir preferred social justice policies on universities. These impositions, however, have often been welcomed by university administrators and academics who believe that universities may be used as instruments of social engineering aimed at solving persistent ills in the wider society. This remodeling adversely affects the proper function of the university.

I have already indicated that there is increased government pressure to graduate more students, even though they may be deficient in knowledge or maturity. This result-oriented approach is favoured by many educational policymakers and trendsetters who are more concerned about the number of graduates than about their quality. Most universities have clear guidelines on the total number of students who will be expected to pass examinations and graduate. Of course, guidelines, by their very nature, are not enforceable or mandatory. Nevertheless, adherence to these guidelines is virtually compulsory because academics, whose pass rates or distribution of grades do not reflect the desirable or appropriate outcome, may be called upon by their university administrators to explain any deviations from these guidelines. Hence, if my experience is an indication, most academics conscientiously adhere to these guidelines, if only to avoid unpleasantness. I have always thought that these guidelines were a means to ensure that enough people would graduate especially since the number provided for failures is extremely small. I was amazed and puzzled recently to read in

University News that, "guidelines for the distribution of grades ... attempt to combat grade inflation, a sure sign of eroding standards."

My dissatisfaction with the present fascination with numbers rather than quality stems from the fact that universities are supposed to be centres of excellence, where the achievement and retention of certain standards are, or ought to be, fostered as ends in themselves. Those who are familiar with the history of universities know that they were established, using the language of John Henry Newman, to employ themselves "in the education of the intellect". He argued in his seminal book *The Idea of a University* that universities should facilitate the forming of a habit of mind "of which the attributes are, freedom, equitableness, calmness, moderation, and wisdom".[39] Thus, universities, their academics and students should ideally possess a genuine desire to pursue truth and should strive to maintain standards of excellence.

---

39 J H C Newman, *The Idea of a University* (new impression), Longmans, Green and Co., London, 1925, 53.

8

REFLECTIONS ON AN AMERICAN SABBATICAL:
DIVERSITY AND FREE SPEECH
(1992)

1. The American law school landscape

The writing of this paper gives me an opportunity to reflect upon my American sabbatical at the University of Notre Dame in 1992. Reflections, usually, do not involve the discussion of rigidly structured arguments but, instead, are "thoughts" about events that have taken place while I was in the United States. These thoughts, at first glance, may appear to be unrelated. Nevertheless, towards the end of my reflections, I propose to draw some tentative conclusions from my thoughts. These conclusions may improve an overall understanding of the inter-relatedness of the issues which I propose to discuss in this paper.

I spent the first semester at the University of Notre Dame Law School which is located at the edge of the City of South Bend in the north of Indiana and only a few miles from the Michigan border. In the latest U.S. News survey on American law schools, Notre Dame was ranked number 24. Although this represents a drop of 5 places on the 1990 survey, it still means that Notre Dame is part of that elitist group of the top 25 law schools in the United States. There are 175 accredited law schools in the United States.

The facilities at the Notre Dame Law School are excellent. Perhaps, it is worth mentioning that the Notre Dame Law School Library is open on a 24-hour basis and there are always industrious and conscientious law students who avail themselves of the opportunity to work in the library at night. I was surprised to discover that the library did not have a security gate or electronic scanner or any other gadgetry to prevent people from removing unregistered books. The librarian assumes that students and staff will not take unregistered books from the library and that they will dutifully and promptly return books which may also be needed by other library users. This honour system seems to work reasonably well. I did not come across damaged or mutilated books with missing pages. In contrast, the Harrison Library of the T C Beirne School of Law, The University of Queensland holds a few books which have been slashed and lacerated by unscrupulous library users. I should hasten to add that the Notre Dame Law School building, including the library, is open to the public between the hours of 8 am and 5 pm. Those who have a legitimate reason for being in the building after 5 pm, for example students and staff, are supplied with keys which provide access to the library and the toilets (or restrooms as they are called in the United States).

American law academics are paid substantially more than in Australia. Full professors at Notre Dame earn in the vicinity of

US$110,000 (approximately AU$140,000). This is a reasonably attractive salary because the City of South Bend where Notre Dame is located, is in a relatively inexpensive part of the United States. At Notre Dame, the starting salary of Assistant Professors of Law (Lecturers) is usually around US$57,000 (approximately AU$70,000). My comments only apply to law academics. Humanities Professors, for example, are paid substantially less than law academics. But apparently the Law School and the University authorities have decided that, if the Law School is to attract and keep suitably qualified law teachers, it must pay them salaries that the market dictates. According to recently released figures, a capable and hard-working graduate, if employed by a big city law firm, earns around US$55,000 during their first year of practice. Lawyers, including academic lawyers, are likely to be in the top five per cent of the income distribution of one of the richest nations in the world. There is, of course, no government agency in the United States that enforces a rigidly regulated salary structure like we have in Australia. In my opinion, national pay scales should be abolished and pay should be linked to performance (or lack of it).

Law academics, at least at Notre Dame, are paid for nine months only. Although a law academic's salary could obviously be disbursed over a period of twelve months, the University has chosen to pay it over a 9-months period. During the three summer months, academics, apart from an obligation to prepare for the next Fall Semester, have no duties and no allegiance to the University. I think that this system is not without merit. Indeed, as law teachers are paid for nine months, they are encouraged to seek outside funds to supplement their incomes. Some choose to seek research funds whilst others may accept summer appointments at nearly colleges or universities. Some even work in South Bend or Chicago law firms for the duration of the summer. I suggest that the system of payment adopted by the University has the effect of encouraging law academics to supplement their university salaries. This system may well contribute, albeit in a small way, to an improvement in the productivity of law teachers, or in a diversification of their skills.

2. The diversity debate

During my time at Notre Dame, several interesting national debates took place. I propose to report on two of these. The most important debate concerned the concept of "diversity." Even a casual visitor to an American campus these days cannot fail to notice the emphasis placed by University administrators on the concept of "diversity". What does it mean? It means that groups in society must be represented among the student body (and the employees, including faculty and staff) in accordance with their numerical strength in the recruitment area of the University. Diversity means proportionality: if blacks constitute 20% of the population of the University's recruitment area, then 20% of its students and staff must be blacks. Thus, universities regard proportional representation "as a just distribution of educational opportunities in a democratic society, where each group is entitled to its share of seats in the freshman class."[40] Of course, if the student body is selected on the basis of the race, gender or sexual orientation of their students, then the traditional principle of merit-based admission is endangered. This traditional or conventional principle of merit attaches primary importance to test scores and grade point averages but also weighs extracurricular activities, when assessing a person's preparation for University study. Universities, of course, have not abandoned the merit system altogether. They continue to apply

---

40 Dinesh D'Souza, *Illiberal Education. The Politics of Race and Sex on Campus*, The Free Press, New York, 1991, 26.

merit criteria but only to measure differences in academic preparation within groups, thereby limiting competition for scarce educational resources to members of the same racial or ethnic group. Thus, blacks compete against other black applicants and Hispanics compete against other Hispanics, but they do not compete against members of other groups. An individual's opportunities very much depend upon one's group membership. "Groups" are chosen on several rational and irrational grounds. Usually, Asians are not considered as a disadvantaged group because they are over-represented in the university population. However, following representations made by members of the Filipino group, Filipinos, at least at Berkeley, are now shielded from competition with white applicants.

Usually, three reasons are adduced for the introduction of this policy of diversity or proportionality. First, proponents of this policy argue that universities serve a democratic society and, therefore, its membership should reflect that society. On this line of argument, a policy of diversity or proportional representation seeks to ensure the participation of all groups in the life of universities. This argument implies that the concept of academic excellence is undemocratic. The second argument involves the claim that the diversity policy compensates for past discrimination by whites against blacks (and other groups). The third argument concentrates on the apparent need in American society of role models: in increasing the number of blacks in colleges and universities, other members of the same group will be encouraged to emulate the achievements of those who are admitted.

An American commentator, Mr D'Souza (and Indian, who came to the United States as an exchange student in the late 70s and who works for the American Enterprise Institute) has recently undertaken a relevant study, the results of which were released while I was at Notre Dame. He argues that, whilst Universities proudly announce, each Fall, that they have been able to increase the representation of minorities on their campuses, they conveniently fail to mention how many of these students graduate. Apparently, incontrovertible statistics indicate that only 25% of these students finish their studies, whereas the passing grade for majority students is considerably higher. Many minority students are not able to contribute to, or to profit from, their involvement with the colleges and universities with which they are matched. This is not to suggest that these minority students are unqualified or stupid. Many have respectable grades and would competently and satisfactorily perform if they had been matched with a less competitive school.

The D'Souza study reveals that the proponents of the diversity policy assume that its implementation results in an increase in the number of minority members on campus. However, he observes that the implementation of a policy of diversity simply increases the competition between universities to attract a significant number of minority students. Indeed, many universities, to attract minority members, offer substantial benefits to these students. These efforts, however, do not increase the overall number of minority members in universities. The failure of these efforts is due to the existence of the "pushing-up" phenomenon which means that blacks who are admitted to Harvard or Yale, would have done admirably well at Irvine, South Carolina, Iowa or another less competitive school. Those who are admitted to Irvine would have done well in a Community College. D'Souza also argued that the policy of diversity inevitably creates ethnic and racial conflicts because groups which benefit under this policy will be envied by majority members who will view minority achievements or non-performance as the products of a preferential admission programme. He concludes that racial division "is the natural consequence of principles that exalt group equality above individual justice."[41]

Issues relating to "diversity" are difficult to talk about in the United States, especially because universities, almost without exception, continue to claim that preferential hiring does not take place. Those who dare to question the prevailing policy of diversity are ostracised and harassed. An example is the story of Timothy Maguire at Georgetown University Law Center. Maguire was a third-year law student, who had worked part-time in the law school's admission office. He stumbled across data which proved that the test scores and grade averages of black students admitted to the Law School were substantially lower than those of white students. He published his data in the School's *Law Weekly*. There was a storm of protests. The University is now threatening to withdraw his law degree that he earned and has also accused him of divulging confidential information. Also, the Law School authorities proposed to deny the editors of the *Law Weekly*, who published the story, their law degrees. I find the proposed Law School action appalling and abhorrent. In my opinion, the Maguire story is a particularly pernicious and odious denial of a student's academic freedom. In my opinion, it should be possible at universities to discuss all kinds of views without fear or favour, including those which the university authorities do not want to hear.

At Notre Dame, I attended a lecture by D'Souza which was part of his tour to promote his book. During question time someone in the audience strongly insisted that Maguire is a criminal and should be in jail, presumably because he had disclosed confidential information. I do not agree. After all, Maguire did not mention any names in his article, but only released statistical information. Also, he brought into the open an issue, the discussion of which

---

41 *Ibid.*, 51.

is studiously avoided by university authorities but is of immense importance for society. Therefore, these issues must for the good of the United States be discussed freely. These issues include the question whether and if so, to what extent, a person's opportunities will be determined by one's race, sex or sexual orientation, the relationship between educational quality and diversity and the question whether a social agenda is improperly intruding in the academic domain. Nevertheless, the diversity movement appears to be unstoppable and has the unqualified support of the overwhelming majority of University Presidents. For example, in a two-page paid advertisement, the President of Notre Dame, argued in the independent student newspaper, *The Observer*, that, "we must dispel once and for all the notion that ethnic minority students are here, as it were, under false pretenses."[42] This opinion expressed by the University's highest executive officer, implies that academics, and indeed, all those associated with the University should desist from the kind of research that Maguire conducted.

The President's statement on diversity was released following the occupation of the University's Administration building by Students United for Respect (SUFR), who had demanded a University statement on the issue of diversity. In his statement, the President thanked these students "who in recent months have held the University accountable for what they perceive to be a lack of progress with regard to cultural diversity."[43] At Notre Dame, a Catholic University, the SUFR students had also demanded that a sufficient number of non-Catholics be admitted to the University and that following their admission the University deemphasises its Catholic traditions in order not to offend the sensitivities of these students. The President, in his diversity statement said that the University, whilst it will continue to serve its Catholic

---
42   *The Observer*, Monday, 29 April 1991, 16.
43   *Ibid.*, 16.

constituency, "must be more successful" in its "pastoral ministry to those of other faith traditions."[44]

The diversity policy is aggressively applied in the recruitment of faculty and other staff of American universities. Most advertisements specifically state that minority candidates and women are particularly encouraged to apply. Recently, Harvard University Law School was sued by some students for employment discrimination because the School had failed to hire enough women, Latinos, Native Americans, Asians, disabled and homosexual professors. Although it will be difficult to prove a causal relationship between the appointments policy of the Law School and the perceived lack of black employment opportunities, the suit is symptomatic of what is happening in the United States. It is ironic that these students use their litigation training to attack the institution that provided them with the training in the first place.

3. Restrictive speech codes

A second, but related issue involves the adoption, by most Universities and Colleges, of restrictive speech codes. For example, the University of Pennsylvania speech code prohibits "ethnic harassment" which is defined as "any behaviour, verbal or physical, that stigmatizes or victimizes individuals." A person is guilty of ethnic harassment if he or she makes a statement to the effect that the victimised person is never going to make it in American society or in his chosen profession because he speaks with an accent.[45] Other speech codes give as examples of prohibited discriminatory behaviour "inappropriately directed laughter" or the non-inclusion of a person in a debate.

---

44 *Ibid.*, 16.
45 *Supra* n. 40, 146.

By way of example I would like to briefly discuss the University of Michigan's speech code, which was invalidated by a United States District Court as involving an unconstitutional abridgment of a person's right to free speech protected by the First Amendment. The University of Michigan speech code prohibits any behaviour, "verbal or physical, that stigmatizes or victimizes an individual on the basis of race, ethnicity, religion, sex, sexual orientation, creed, national origin, ancestry, age, marital status, handicap or Vietnam-era veteran status." The University Office of Affirmative Action issued an interpretive and authoritative interpretation of the Policy and provided examples of sanctionable conduct. These included:

> A male student makes remarks in class like 'Women just aren't as good in this field as men,' thus creating a hostile learning atmosphere for female classmates. Students in a residence hall have a floor party and invite everyone on their floor except one person because they think she might be a lesbian. Two men demand that their roommate in the residence hall move out and be tested for AIDS. You display a confederate flag on the door of your room in the residence hall. You laugh at a joke about someone in your class who stutters.

The University's speech code, officially known as Policy on Discrimination and Discriminatory Harassment of Students in the University Environment was challenged by a Psychology graduate student in *Doe v University of Michigan*.[46] The applicant, Mr Doe (a pseudonym to preserve his privacy) challenged the constitutionality of the Policy. Mr Doe specialised in the interdisciplinary study of biological bases of individual differences in personality traits and mental abilities. He argued that, "certain controversial theories positing biologically-based differences between sexes and races might be perceived as 'sexist' and 'racist' by some students, and

---

46 721 F.Supp. 852 (E.D. Mich. 1989).

he feared that discussion of such theories might be sanctionable under the Policy."⁴⁷ His fears were reinforced when a student was subjected to a formal hearing provided for under the Policy, because he had expressed his belief, in the context of a social work research class, that homosexuality was a disease that could be psychologically treated.

The District Judge decided that although the University could legitimately regulate so-called "fighting words", which by their very utterance tend to incite an immediate breach of the peace, it cannot prohibit the public expression of ideas solely because they are offensive to their hearers. The Judge's view on this issue is sound in the light of the Supreme Court's recent statement that if "there is a bedrock principle underlying the First Amendment, it is that the Government may not prohibit the expression of an idea simply because society finds the idea itself offensive or disagreeable."⁴⁸ According to the Judge, the public expression of ideas has "a special significance in the university setting, where the free and unfettered interplay of competing views is essential to the institution's educational mission."⁴⁹ He held that the Policy, in as far as it restricted the right of the plaintiff to express his views, was unconstitutional because of overbreadth and vagueness. The Policy applied to speech that is constitutionally protected speech and the language of the Policy made it virtually impossible to predict which statements would be deemed to violate the Policy. Thus, the Judge condemned the Policy because committing the offence of discriminatory harassment did not so much depend on the intention of the offender as on its perceived effect on the victim. D'Souza reports in his book that the University of Michigan, despite this Court decision, nevertheless continues "to attempt to devise new

---

47 *Ibid.* n. 46., 858.
48 *Texas v Johnson*, 491 US 397 (1989) (per Brennan J).
49 *Supra.* n. 46, 863.

policies that would survive First Amendment challenge while still restricting offensive expression" and that "a university that was once dedicated to maximum freedom of mind and conscience now finds itself struggling to guarantee the minimum freedom insisted on by the law."[50] He concludes that the "efforts of the administration at Michigan and other schools to regulate and enforce a social etiquette have created an enormous artificiality of discourse among peers, and thus have become an obstacle to that true openness that seems to be the only sure footing for equality."[51]

4. The political correctness movement

Attempts to harness a person's free speech is part of the Political Correctness movement, currently sweeping American campuses. This movement aims at prohibiting discussion of sensitive, yet important social and moral issues which does not accord with the anti-discrimination, pro-diversity, and feminist views of present university policymakers. The movement puts into effect the advice of Herbert Marcuse who in well-known essay on *Critique of Pure Tolerance* condoned the "withdrawal of toleration of speech and assembly from groups and movements which promote aggressive policies, armament, chauvinism, discrimination on grounds of race and religion or which oppose the extension of public services, social security and medical care."[52] In line with the Political Correctness philosophy, it is not unusual for universities to require its students and staff to attend compulsory sensitivity training programmes. The spring 1991 issue of *Campus*, America's student newspaper reports that a senior manager in the Duke University Medical Center had been suspended for four weeks without pay

---

50 *Supra* n. 40, 144.
51 *Supra* n. 40, 156.
52 Herbert Marcuse, *Critique of Pure Tolerance*, Beacon Press, Boston, 1965, 100.

because he had referred to a job applicant as a homosexual after observing their mannerism during the application interview. To be considered for reinstatement, the University required him to compulsorily attend a course designed to heighten his sensitivity toward gender issues. In addition, he was compelled to perform volunteer service for an organisation that promotes tolerance in the community. In another incident, a faculty member at the University of Missouri was accused of being a racist because he had criticised Supreme Court Justice Thurgood Marshall in a lecture. These examples are not isolated events but are part of what I regard as a disturbing and appalling trend towards the imposition of politically correct views on students and staff. In my opinion, such imposition is incompatible with the idea of a University as a place where even unpopular and idiosyncratic views should be discussed without fear or favour.

5. Is there a message in nudity?

The Doe case, of course, is only one case among many dealing with the First Amendment to the United States Constitution.[53] Although the First Amendment has been interpreted innumerable times, an authoritative interpretation has eluded the courts. Recently, American courts have again had occasion to consider the free speech clause of the First Amendment. These cases involve the contentious issue of whether nude barroom dancing is protected speech. This issue is considered by both the 7th and 8th Circuit Courts in *Miller v Civil City of South Bend*[54] and *Walker v City of Kansas*

---

53 The First Amendment to the United States Constitution proclaims that, "Congress shall make no law respecting an establishment of religion or prohibiting the free exercise thereof; or abridging the freedom of speech, or of the press, or the right of the people peaceably to assemble, and to petition the Government for a redress of grievances."
54 904 F.2d 1081 (7th Cir. 1990).

*City, Mo.*⁵⁵ respectively.

An analysis of recent free speech jurisprudence reveals that, usually, courts make a distinction between "speech" and "conduct". If nude dancing is speech, it is protected by the Constitution. However, if it is conduct, then it can be regulated. Of course, there is a fine line between speech and conduct. This stems from the fact that speech usually involves expression, which is action. The Constitution also protects expressive conduct which is sometimes referred to as "symbolic speech". A paradigm example of symbolic speech is the case of *Tinker v Des Moines Independent Community School District*[56] which involved high school students who decided to wear black armbands in school to protest the war in Vietnam, despite a school regulation which prohibited such conduct. But non-expressive conduct is not protected by the Constitution. But even if nude dancing is deemed to constitute protected speech, the time, place, and manner of its exercise may still be regulated. For example, solicitation or begging may be regulated; its constitutionality will depend upon the type of forum in which it takes place. If the regulation is content-based, namely intended to suppress the views of an unpopular group, it would be unconstitutional.[57] In *Ward v Rock Against Racism*,[58] the Supreme Court examined the constitutionality of a municipal noise regulation that was challenged by a group of musicians who wished to use a louder sound system in a public bandshell. The Court stated that the "principal inquiry in determining content neutrality in speech cases generally, and in time, place, or manner cases in particular, is whether the government has adopted a regulation of speech because of disagreement with the message it conveys" and that a "regulation that serves

---

55   911 F.2d 80 (8th Cir. 1990).
56   393 US 503 (1969).
57   *United States v Kokinda*, 497 US 720 (1990).
58   491 US 781 (1989).

purposes unrelated to the content of expression is deemed neutral, even if it has an incidental effect on some speakers or message, but not others."[59] The regulation must also be necessary, thus narrowly tailored to the government's interest. Is it a complete ban on free speech or could the government objectives be achieved by a partial ban? The regulation must also leave open adequate alternative avenues for expression.

Is nude barroom dancing expressive conduct? In this context it may be necessary to consider whether nude dancing conveys a particularised message and whether there is a likelihood that the message would be understood by those who receive it. It may be argued that the question should be answered in the negative considering the Supreme Court decision in *City of Dallas v Stanglin*.[60] In *Stanglin*, the Supreme Court considered the associational rights of minors who were being excluded from dance halls. In holding that dance hall patrons were not engaged in any form of expressive conduct, it stated that, "it is possible to find some kernel of expression in almost every activity a person undertakes – for example, walking down the street or meeting one's friend at a shopping mall – but such a kernel is not sufficient to bring the activity within the protection of the First Amendment".[61] Thus, the Supreme Court acknowledged that all activities do not qualify for the protection of the First Amendment; some activity is merely conduct which is not expressive.

In *Miller*, most judges of the 7th Circuit held that non-obscene barroom variety nude dancing performed as entertainment is expressive conduct and, as such, entitled to protection under the First Amendment. *Miller* involved a drinking establishment in the

---

59 Ibid., 791.
60 490 US 19 (1989).
61 Ibid., 25.

City of South Bend, the Kitty Kat Lounge. Kitty Kat provided nude dancing as entertainment for their patrons. The Court opined that, "While clearly not all conduct is expression, dance as entertainment is a form of conduct that is inherently expressive."[62] It involves the communication of emotion or ideas. Furthermore, the Court reasoned that any attempt to distinguish between "low" and "high" art cannot be made for constitutional purposes. Thus, no distinction could be made between the seductive nudity of Salome in Strauss's opera and the vulgar nudity of a nude dancer in Kitty Kat. The Court admitted, though, that the State is not powerless to regulate the presentation of nude dancing: in fact, the State retains a great deal of control, but the regulation must constitute a reasonable time, place and manner restriction on protected expression. Judge Cudahy, concurring in the judgment argued that barroom striptease is expressive because "a striptease sends an unadorned message to a male audience. It is a message of temptation and allurement coupled with coy hints at satisfaction."[63]

By far the most interesting majority opinion was written by Judge Posner. His opinion is by any standards a *tour de force*: it is mightily entertaining as well as intellectually stimulating. It is an opinion which combines intellectual rigour and erudition with clarity and literary prowess. Among other things, he penned this memorable passage:

> Erotic dances express exotic emotion, such as sexual excitement and longing. Nudity is the usual state in which sexual intercourse is conducted in our culture, and disrobing is preliminary to nudity. But of course nudity and disrobing are not *invariably* associated with sex The goal of the striptease – a goal to which the dancing is indispensable – is to enforce the asso-

---

62   *Supra* n. 54, 1085.
63   *Supra* n. 54, 1089.

ciation: to make plain that the performer is not removing her clothes because she is about to take a bath or change into another set of clothes or undergo a medical examination; to insinuate that she is removing them because she is preparing for, thinking about, and desiring sex. The dance ends when the preparations are complete. The sequel is left to the viewer's imagination This is the "tease" in "striptease".[64]

He analytically discusses a few objections to the claim that nude barroom dancing constitutes expressive conduct. First, it could be argued that, if nude dancing is expressive conduct, then every activity could potentially qualify, for example, slamming a door as a sign that one is angry. But according to Posner, the expression which is protected by the First Amendment is the expression of a thought sensation, or emotion to another person or persons. Second, it may be claimed that nude dancing is simply not the type of message protected by the Constitution: what is protected is the expression of ideas or opinions. He points out that if the only expression that the First Amendment protects is the expression of ideas and opinions, then most music and visual art, and much of literature, are unprotected. This would be a shockingly inadequate interpretation of the First Amendment as it has come to be understood. If the only way to exclude nude dancing from the protection of the First Amendment is to exclude all non-political art and literature as well, the price is too high.

Posner's opinion was the subject of attack by the minority judges. For example, Judge Easterbrook opines that, "James Madison would have guffawed had anyone suggested public nudity as an example of 'freedom of speech' – or of anything that could be derived from the Framers' conception by a series of plausible interpretations."[65] Judge Easterbrook argues that, even if nude

---

64 *Supra* n. 54, 1091.
65 *Supra* n. 54, 1124.

barroom dancing is protected speech, the Indiana legislation would still have been constitutional because it is content-neutral legislation that only incidentally burdens speech. For him, it is necessary to examine whether the purpose of the legislation is to suppress communication. The minority also accuses the majority of judicial law-making. In this context, Easterbrook J argues that concern "about the limits of *judicial* power, about the authority for an official with life tenure to countermand a decision of the elected legislature, must be at the forefront in every constitutional case."[66] Judge Manion, in his dissent, argues that Constitutions may be changed by the people but not the judges. He adds that the people would almost certainly not support a Constitutional amendment which says that the right of citizens to entertain by dancing nude in public shall not be denied or abridged by the United States or by any State. Yet, it is precisely such amendment of the Constitution that in this case is achieved by a handful of judges who are not accountable to the public. However, in his judgment, Posner J suggests that the "original understanding as a guide to constitutional interpretation" changes the Constitution from a "living document into a petrified reminder of the limits of human foresight."[67] Judge Posner is simply restating the message which is constantly, but perhaps uncritically, being heard in American and Australian constitutional law classes, namely that the Constitution is a living document which has to be interpreted in the light of present circumstances, thereby justifying decisions which no doubt would have been abhorrent to the drafters of the Constitution.

In my opinion, it could be argued that the majority's decision is seductively appealing. It is based on the libertarian, Millian understanding of the law and human nature. According to this

---

66 *Supra* n. 54, 1131.
67 *Supra* n. 54, 1096.

understanding, the law should only interfere in people's freedom if the exercise of that freedom is likely to result in harm to others. Nevertheless, such understanding does not promote what I would call the "democratic legitimacy" of judicial decisions. A determination of the wisdom, need, or propriety of laws is the role of an elected legislature, not the judiciary. The need to practice judicial restraint must have been in the mind of Justice Holmes when he stated in *Hudson County Water Co. v McCarter*[68] that there is a tendency of "All rights ... to declare themselves absolute to their logical extreme."[69] In the same vein, Chief Justice Burger made the following remarks in 1973 in *United States v 12,200-Ft. Reels of Film*:[70]

> The seductive plausibility of single steps in a chain of evolutionary development of a legal rule is often not perceived until a third, fourth, or fifth logical extension occurs. Each step, when taken, appeared a reasonable step in relation to that which preceded it, although the aggregate or end result is one that would never have been seriously considered in the first instance. This kind of gestative propensity calls for the 'line drawing' familiar in the judicial, as in the legislative process – 'thus far but not beyond'.[71]

In *Walker*, the 8th Circuit decided that nude dancing is not protected speech. The Court's argument focussed on *Stanglin*, where it was decided that ballroom dancing is not protected by the Constitution. The Court said that, "it turns the Supreme Court's First Amendment rulings on their heads to maintain that an activity unprotected by the First Amendment when the participants are clothed acquires exalted status under that amendment if the participants shed their clothes."[72]

---

68 209 US 349 (1908).
69 *Ibid.*, 355.
70 413 US 123 (1973).
71 *Ibid.*, 127.
72 *Supra* n. 55, 89.

The apparent incompatibility between the 7th and 8th Circuits may well necessitate an authoritative decision by the Supreme Court on this issue. Although it is always difficult to predict how the Court would rule on any given issue, it is possible to predict that the Indiana-nudity law will survive.[73] I base my opinion on a recent case, *Employment Division., Department of Human Resources of Oregon. v Smith*[74] in which the Supreme Court held that generally applicable government regulations will survive a challenge on First Amendment grounds despite the expressive characteristics of the activity. Indeed, the court is unwilling to protect certain religious free exercise and journalistic opinion against state regulation. Specifically, in *Smith*, the Supreme Court decided that the State of Oregon can criminally prosecute two adherents of the Native American Church for ingesting peyote notwithstanding their claim that the Statute infringed their free exercise rights. This case is significant because the reasoning of Justice Scalia for the majority indicates that, provided a statute is neutral on its face and generally applicable, it may be applied, without compelling justification, notwithstanding the claim that it infringes on religious practice. Thus, under this view, Catholics would have had no right to a constitutional exemption for the consumption of wine during the Prohibition era. In fact, Catholics did obtain a statutory exemption.

6. Concluding comments

---

[73] The Supreme Court reversed *Miller* in *Barnes v Glen Theatre, Inc.*, 501 US 560 (1991), 567-568 where Rhenquist CJ stated that, "we find that Indiana's public indecency statute is justified despite its incidental limitations on some expressive activity. The public indecency statute is clearly within the constitutional power of the State, and furthers substantial governmental interests. ... the statute's purpose of protecting societal order and morality is clear from its text and history."

[74] 494 US 872 (1990).

What conclusions could possibly be drawn from these two inter-related issues discussed in this paper, namely diversity and free speech? Although it may be unwarranted to draw any sweeping conclusions, there is always a desire to understand the totality of events that take place in society or, indeed, the world. The diversity and free speech issues, in my opinion, illustrate the existence in contemporary America of two, but largely incompatible, approaches to the protection of constitutionally protected rights. The diversity issue suggests that rights depend upon group membership and that any criticism of this approach will be viewed as an abuse of a person's right to freedom of speech. Freedom of speech, although constitutionally protected, is under threat from the political correctness movement, even in a university context. In contrast, the individual approach to freedom of speech prevailed in the nudity cases.

A society where every individual is free to pursue his or her own objectives without interference or restrictions is, in an ideal world, the best society. Such a society would need to be tempered with compassion and the realisation that not all people are able to take advantage of the opportunities that society has to offer.

9

THE NEW ETHNIC CONSCIOUSNESS:
A NATIONAL LANGUAGE POLICY FOR A MULTICULTURAL AUSTRALIA?
(1993)

1. Language as a symbol of ethnicity

Issues dealing with the protection of linguistic minorities have been studied systematically by scholars for at least two hundred years. In the relevant literature, a discussion of these issues often figures prominently in the context of an analysis of the concept "ethnicity". Indeed, "language" is invariably described as the "most salient symbol of ethnicity because it carries the past and expresses present and future attitudes and aspirations."[75] If "language" is the most salient symbol of ethnicity, then any resurgence of ethnicity

---

75 H Giles, "Introductory Essay" in H Giles (ed.) *Language, Ethnicity and Intergroup Relations*, London, Academic Press, 1977, 4. See also J A Fishman, "Language and Ethnicity" in H Giles (ed.), in *Language, Ethnicity and Intergroup Relations*, 15-17.

may be expected to be linked, at least in part, to language issues. Thus, a commentator on ethnic and linguistic issues, Professor J A Fishman, wrote in 1976 that, "larger number of individuals, in Western as well as in non-Western societies, have recently recognised and even stressed their ethnicity more than was the case just a few years ago"[76] and he suggested that this rebirth of ethnicity is inextricably linked to the increased concern for the protection of linguistic minorities. He went on to say that the "assumed link between language and ethnicity is an absolute desideratum if we are to fathom any collectivity's reactions to the use or non-use of its language in ritual, in official/governmental domains, in education ... or its reactions to language planning ... or to the admission of languages of wider communication (such as English) into various domains of social behaviour."[77] A language is thus vastly more than a means of communication: It is also a powerful symbol of ethnicity. As such, it expresses or evokes several other characteristics which an individual is deemed to possess as a member of an ethnic group. Thus, it is not surprising that one's native language is often assumed to be conclusive evidence of the possession of certain other characteristics, which all the members of the language group are deemed to possess.

In this paper, I propose to argue that the uncritical acceptance of the proposition that one's native language is indicative of membership in an ethnic group, is largely responsible for the increasing incidence of ethnic conflicts in recent times. These conflicts arise (or are exacerbated) when self-proclaimed or chosen leaders of ethnic groups incorrectly assume that all people who share a common native language will loyally support demands for a redistribution of political, economic and social power and a greater share of society's resources. It is not unexpected, however, that the proposition

---
[76] Fishman, *supra* n. 75, 15.
[77] Fishman, *supra* n. 75, 15.

continues to be treated as self-evident and valid. This stems from the fact that, as I will argue in the next section, the demonstrable improvement in the political and social fortunes of linguistic minorities has been facilitated by the belief that language is, indeed, a proxy for other characteristics which all people who share a common language are deemed to possess.

2. The protection of linguistic minorities and the rise of Nation States in Europe

Even a perfunctory survey of European ethnic groups reveals that, during the last two hundred years, these groups have moved towards self-determination and political and/or cultural autonomy. This development, which started after the French Revolution, involved the idea that each ethnic group was entitled to have its own state and that each state is to be based on one ethnic group. Thus, it is common knowledge among all those who are even remotely interested in European affairs, that the nineteenth century saw the unifications of Germany and of Italy. These unifications are important developments because due to the existence of several German/Italian mini States prior to unification, Germans/Italians, even though they arguably belonged to the same ethnic group, did not share the same German/Italian nation state. This demand for self-determination and for the coincidence of ethnic groups with States, was not limited to these regions. In fact, the trend was so strong that the major changes decided upon by the victorious powers after the First World War resulted in the redrawing of State boundaries which were more in line with the geographical distribution of ethnic groups Two commentators, Joroslav Krejci and Vitezslaw Velimsky pointed out in their book *Ethnic and Political*

Nations in Europe[78] that, "As a result of the redrawing of boundaries the percentage of population belonging to ethnic nations without state or self-government in Europe decreased from about 26 per cent in 1910 to only about 7 per cent in 1930."[79] Further adjustments were made after the Second World War when large-scale transfer of populations and territorial changes took place. Krejci and Velimsky conclude that, "All these changes further reduced the significance of the ethnic minorities throughout Europe" and "that the share of ethnic minorities not accommodated by any such arrangement decreased to about 3 per cent of the European population."[80] The redrawing of the boundaries was facilitated also by a rebirth of nationalism, defined as a desire to promote the strength and ambitions of the ethnic nations of which one was a member. As indicated before, languages served as prominent symbols of the reawakened aspirations of ethnic groups.

These efforts, aimed at minimising the difference between ethnic groups and States, were not limited to large-scale compulsory population transfers and a redrawing of boundaries. Indeed, some European States considered the ethnic aspirations of their peoples also by constitutional arrangements which aimed at granting equal partnership status to ethnic groups which had been neglected in the past. For example, in the nineteenth century there were some constitutional changes in Central Europe which were instrumental in harmonising the demands of ethnic groups with the requirements of statehood. At present, similar constitutional developments are taking place in Belgium and Spain. It is impossible, within the scope of this paper to describe these constitutional arrangements. It suffices to say that, in the main, these changes aspire at bringing about a social order based on some conception

---

[78] J Krejci and V Velimsky, *Ethnic and Political Nations in Europe*, London, Croom Helm, 1981.
[79] *Ibid.*, 63.
[80] *Ibid.*, 64.

of guaranteed political representation within society. For example, these internal arrangements may require equal representation for each ethnic group, including linguistic and other minority groups in society, on decision-making forums. Professor Nathan Glazer, in describing a number of such constitutional arrangements, argues that these arrangements are not necessarily seen as compensation for past societal discrimination of one group against another group, but are usually justified on utilitarian grounds, including the claim that they may contribute to a "stable political balance in a deeply divided country" and are a necessary requirement for the maintenance of a "democratic and just social order."[81]

My brief overview of ethno-political relations in Europe reveals that the aspirations of ethnic groups for self-determination have been fulfilled to a large extent. Indeed, as already indicated, European States gradually reconciled themselves with the presence and the aspirations of their ethnic groups through large-scale population transfers and redrawing of State boundaries and through constitutional arrangements. Of course, the increased protection for ethnic groups did not shield Europe against the Second World War and, therefore, did not necessarily contribute to an increased awareness of the necessity of ethnic tolerance and co-operation among nations. The protection of ethnic groups is, at least in part, a consequence of nationalism which often involves extreme positions and claims of cultural and linguistic superiority. Also, a brief study of the European population transfers reveals that these transfers involved, or were accompanied with, great personal tragedies and hardships. But, in this paper, I do not propose to discuss the question whether these transfers have resulted in a "better" Europe. My observations concentrate on the point that ethnic groups

---

81 N Glazer, "Individualism and Equality in the United States", in H J Gans, N Glazer, J R Gusfield and C Jencks (eds.), *On the Making of Americans: Essays in Honor of David Riesman*, University of Pennsylvania Press, 1979, 137.

attained political and/or cultural independence in the sense that the difference between ethnic groups and States were gradually reduced, thereby bringing about greater internal protection for these groups.

3. The rise of a new "ethnic consciousness"

If the progressive identification of ethnic groups with States is an incontestable reality, then it is surprising that nowadays ethnic consciousness is once more a potent force in many European as well as non-European societies, including in Australia. The increase in ethnic consciousness was correctly identified as a paradox by Professor Nathan Glazer when he stated some years ago that, "We have been surprised by the rise of new ethnic or quasi-ethnic identities in those states that were considered either models of contemporary modern nation-states or successes in having subordinated their ethnic divisions to the terminal loyalty of the nation."[82] Of course, students of ethnic affairs would still be able to argue that not all ethnic groups benefited from the readjustments following the two World Wars and that, "some had to see a part of their ethnic community detached and incorporated into another nation state"[83] where they became a minority. Nevertheless, the present interest in ethnicity is disproportionately great compared to the relatively minor problems generated by leaving out some ethnic groups from the new arrangements. Therefore, I suggest that a more satisfactory answer should be found to solve the paradox identified by Professor Glazer. I submit that the paradox arises from the fact that language is often incorrectly used as proxy for other characteristics which are relevant in determining membership in an ethnic group. Thus, one's ability (or inability)

---
82 N Glazer, "Ethnicity: A World Phenomenon", 8, No. 3/4 *Dialogue* 34 (1975), 40.
83 Krejci, *supra* n.78, 70.

to speak a language is taken as conclusive evidence of membership (or non-membership) in an ethnic group, even though a person, despite a common, native language, may not regard himself or herself as a member of such group. Thus, I suggest that the dramatic rise in ethnic consciousness in modern times involves only, to a limited extent, attempts by ethnic groups to obtain political and/or cultural autonomy, and is more a result of an increasing demand made by persons, either individually or in conjunction with other individuals, to be exempted from membership in a particular group, even though they are deemed to belong to such group by virtue of a common language.

In Australia, ethnic tensions arise when attempts are made by ethnic leaders to increase the political leverage of ethnic groups by artificially inflating their membership. These attempts are based on the pragmatic consideration that political power is proportionate to the numerical strength of an ethnic group. The total memberships of these groups may be increased artificially if one's native language is deemed to be enough indication or, indeed, conclusive evidence of membership in the group. The ethnic tensions, now prevalent in Australia, could well escalate into open conflict if many people are involuntarily drafted into an ethnic group by leaders who arrogate to themselves the right to speak on their behalf and who frustrate efforts by these people to assimilate with the English-speaking majority. It is fair to suggest that many immigrants who left their homelands for political and economic reasons desire to submerge themselves in the mainstream majority, thereby divesting themselves of their previous ethnic identity. The emergence of a new ethnic consciousness, then, often involves a conflict between group solidarity which is based on a common language, and the rights of persons to be exempted from membership of the group they are deemed to belong to by virtue of a common language.

The issues raised by this conflict are important but, because of constraints on the length of this article, I will only be able to sketch the basic outlines of the present controversy. It could be argued reasonably that efforts to protect ethnic minorities, defined as a collection of people sharing a common language, will be defeated because these efforts are based on the rebuttable assumption that language constitutes conclusive evidence of the possession of other relevant characteristics, relied upon to determine group membership. Ethnic conflicts, then, may arise if some individuals, simply on be basis of a common language, are induced, against their will, to be associated with a group. If language is taken as irrefutable proof of the existence of other characteristics, then this assumption may well result in the violation of the expectations of some persons who do not want to be included as members of the group. Moreover, this issue questions our ability to clearly define the nature of a group and to establish workable guidelines for determining group membership. It is not surprising that discussions about ethnic conflicts today are replete with fallacious reasoning because proponents and opponents of ethnicity too readily assume that a group is a monolithic entity, thereby raising intractable problems entailed in determining group membership.

If my preceding argument is correct, then, in countries like Australia, ethnic problems are caused not so much by efforts of groups to achieve political and/or cultural independence, but are caused by attempts to resist the struggle by persons, either individually or in conjunction with other individuals, to be exempted from membership of the group to which they are deemed to belong by virtue of their possession of a common language. I would like to illustrate this conflict with reference to the debate in Australia about the desirability of establishing a multicultural society.

4. Australian multiculturalism

It is, of course, well-known by ethnicity scholars and by laymen alike that the concept of ethnicity is heatedly debated in Australia. The existence in our society of several ethnic groups has facilitated the non-critical acceptance of declarations, which describe Australia as a "multicultural" society. I have always been perplexed by the apparent ability of some Australians of different ethnic origin to implement a so-called policy on multiculturalism without feeling the need to clarify the concept. This concern with multiculturalism is even more surprising because Australia is, at present, in operational terms, a highly assimilatory society. Indeed, Professor Lauchlan Chipman has pointed out that, "Intermarriage, despite negative pressure ... has occurred at a higher rate than many predicted."[84] Therefore, the frequent assertions that, "assimilation has failed ... and that Australia is a multi-cultural society, are irresponsibly tendentious."[85] A study of the concept of multiculturalism vividly illustrates the conflict which I described in the previous section, namely the aspiration of some persons to be free from membership in a group of which they are deemed to be a member by virtue of a common language.

A study of the concept of multiculturalism reveals that it is often "an irritatingly muddled way of trying to represent the whole range of very different life-styles to be found among Australian residents."[86] In this sense multiculturalism could be taken to refer to the "respect for difference and non-conformity, and the recognition that one's own values and beliefs are neither unique nor infallible."[87] In this sense, multiculturalism is compatible with liberal pluralism. However, the concept of multiculturalism becomes problematic

---

84   L Chipman, "The Menace of Multi-Culturalism", *Quadrant*, October 1980, 4.
85   Ibid., 4.
86   Ibid., 4.
87   Ibid., 4.

if it is interpreted as anti-assimilationism and ethnic separatism, involving, but not limited to, the demand often heard nowadays that linguistic groups have the right to have their own language, and its corresponding values, supported by governments. The assumption that a common native language is conclusive evidence of one's ethnic group membership is a prerequisite for the survival of this latter version of multiculturalism. A successful rebuttal of this assumption infers that some people may consciously seek assimilation with the majority mainstream population. A desire to assimilate, in turn, undermines any legitimate claim to government-funded survival of ethnic languages and cultures. The present emergence of a renewed interest in ethnicity in Australian politics precisely involves a conflict between those interested in promoting assimilation, and those who persistently demand the government-backed development of multiculturalism as a means to wrest further financial advantages and other benefits for, what they believe, are homogeneous linguistic groups. It is fair to say that this latter interpretation of the concept of multiculturalism is increasingly being embraced uncritically by several proponents of multiculturalism in Australia.

I would like to illustrate this assertion with reference to the language policy which was worked out during the National language Policy Conference, held in 1982 in Canberra and which led to a continuing analysis, but unqualified approval, of this policy by the Senate Standing Committee on Education and the Arts, which released its report in October 1984. It was stated in the preamble to the Conference's report that the "challenge of the eighties will be to develop and implement policies which meet the needs of one of the most multicultural nations in the world, whose survival and prosperity depend on harmony in its internal and international relationships" and that, "a National Policy on Languages which acknowledges the need for ... ethnic

... groups, to maintain their languages and culture, and which improves communication both within the Australian community and internationally by encouraging the learning of languages"[88] is central to such multicultural policy. Whilst the first part of the statement, namely that prosperity depends on harmony in international relationships in uncontroversial, the second part according to which the maintenance of languages, other than English, is essential in achieving harmony is a *non sequitur*. Communication in other languages is neither a sufficient nor a necessary requirement for peace and harmony and may well, upon closer investigation, be responsible for strife and friction, the avoidance of which requires reversing this second interpretation of multiculturalism according to which persons are entitled to have their languages and values supported by taxpayers' money. Thus, the concept of multiculturalism is not confined to tolerating the existence of pluralistic values in society but is increasingly being used to put leverage on governments to support actively the maintenance of ethnic or community languages, values and traditions in Australia. A review of the literature pertaining to multiculturalism reveals, however, that proponents of the second version of multiculturalism, in trying to obtain government funds for the maintenance of their languages and values, use arguments which are compatible with the first version of multiculturalism which demands no more than respect for difference and non-conformity in society.

5. A National language policy for a multicultural Australia?

This chameleon-like ability of the concept of multiculturalism obscures the consequences of the policy and the direction in which

---

88 The Federation of Ethnic Communities' Councils of Australia, *National Language Policy Conference Report*, Canberra, 1982, 24.

our society is or should be heading. The Australian debate on multiculturalism should concentrate more on the consequences of the implementation of the policy which has now resulted in increasing demands made on governments to support actively the maintenance of the languages and the values of our ethnic minorities. I can only speculate upon the consequences of this policy of active support. However, a clue could be found in the language policy, worked out during the Language Policy Conference held in Canberra in 1982. The Conference formally resolved that all Australians have "the right to communicate and to have access to information services commensurate to one's needs – and this not as a privilege but a basic right guaranteed by statute."[89] Further, the Conference recommended that, "the vital importance of access to English should not be taken to imply a diminished acceptance of every person's right to maintain the language of the home and the essential importance of language for personal identity" and that governments should enact legislation "to guarantee the rights of all persons in Australia to maintain and develop the languages of their cultures and to guarantee that all persons in Australia have the opportunity to acquire at least one other language."[90] The Conference, in making the recommendations that governments must actively support and maintain languages considered *Lau v Nichols*.[91] In that case, the United States Supreme Court ruled that the San Francisco Unified School District illegally discriminated against 1800 non-English speaking Chinese-American students by failing to help them surmount the language barrier. In requiring these students to attend regular English language classes, the Supreme Court found that the School District had denied them a "meaningful opportunity to participate in the education program."[92] The Court decided that

---

89 *Ibid.*, 16.
90 *Ibid.*, 16.
91 414 US 563 (1974).
92 *Ibid.*, 568 (per Douglas J).

there is "no equality of treatment merely by providing students with the same facilities, textbooks, teachers, and curriculum,"[93] and concluded that, "students who do not understand English are effectively foreclosed from any meaningful education."[94] However, the Court in *Lau* did not establish the principle that ethnic groups are entitled to receive education in their own languages. Indeed, the introduction of bi-lingual education was only a means to help them to assimilate into the American society. Thus, the Court promoted what has become known in the relevant literature as "transitional" multiculturalism "whereby languages other than English, are used in a school only so long as the migrant children have no mastery of English.[95] Professor John Edwards, a scholar in the field of ethnic studies, pointed out that these languages are gradually phased out as soon as they are of no use or hinder the maintenance of a cohesive society. Thus, the American legislator's "concept of bilingual education, in fact appears to be one in which instruction in the mother tongue is provided as a temporary measure until the children are able to move into an all-English curriculum."[96]

Of course, it would be irresponsible to state that the deliberate maintenance of, and support for, ethnic languages by government will lead to a less cohesive society, even though a number of social commentators have suggested that a policy of active support for ethnic languages may inevitably result in a weakening of our society. Paradoxically, the creation of a cohesive society is seen by proponents of this type of multiculturalism as the major benefit

---

93 Ibid., 566.
94 Ibid., 566.
95 J J Smolicz, "Multiculturalism: Reality or Tokenism", in N. Dimitropoulos and M Ghiotsalitis (eds), *Welfare Service Delivery to Greek People in Australia and Inter-Ethnic Group Relations: A Case for Affirmative Action*, Greek-Australian Welfare Workers' Conference, Adelaide, 1983, 37.
96 J Edwards, "Ethnic Identity and Bilingual Education", in H Giles (ed.) *Language, Ethnicity and Intergroup Relations*, London, Academic Press, 1977, 269.

of multicultural policies. If a cohesive society is promoted by policies which result in the maintenance of separate linguistic entities in our society, as opposed to the multiculturalism as a means of providing respect for difference and non-conformity, then it may well necessitate the introduction of formal prescriptions. Indeed, a Polish legal philosopher, Adam Podgorecki has argued that a "social system which is structurally heterogeneous and based on pluralistic values provides, in order to introduce and maintain a stable balance, the members of this society with precise formal prescriptions regulating their social behaviour, changeable only as a result of conflicting social forces."[97] Podgorecki's views are not very controversial because they are supported by strong evidence that prescriptive law flourishes in social systems which are structurally diversified. Indeed, these formal prescriptions become necessary to maintain a stable society. In this sense, language rights would add to the already increasing burdens placed on individuals, requiring conformist social behaviour. Also, it is worth speculating whether support for the maintenance of ethnic languages may, at least in the short term, lead in the market place to the recruitment of members of one group by other members of the same group, with ethnic and linguistic affinities playing the role of a most conspicuous criterion of selection.

These considerations point to the need to examine seriously the question whether, and if so, to what extent, the evolution of an Australian identity is compatible with the existence of, and support for, ethnic core values and languages in Australia. Of course, the right of all residents to speak any conceivable language and to organise themselves collectively to promote these languages and the values associated with them, is not questioned. Indeed, in a democracy, individuals may adopt different methods aimed at or-

---

97 A Podgorecki, Social Systems Versus Legal Systems – Basic Issues, 4 (undated and mimeographed).

ganising their lives freely. However, in view of the possible undesirable effects of a policy of multiculturalism which aims at continued support for ethnic languages, the question may legitimately be asked whether governments should be in the business of according equal status to these languages in Australia. If these questions are not addressed, it cannot possibly be said that now "ethnicity represents an enlightened form of participatory tours-meeting democracy, a breath of fresh air, the logos of the free spirit."[98]

---

98   Fishman, *supra* n. 75, 40.

10

RALPH McINERNY AND THE AUTHORITY OF THE POPE
A RESPONSE TO A LECTURE
(1993)

During the last couple of days, I have approached several people to encourage them to attend Professor Ralph McInerny's lecture tonight.[99] In retrospect, my efforts in this regard were unnecessary because the lecture theatre is completely full. It does not often happen that we have the opportunity, in Brisbane, to listen to an acclaimed lecturer with an international reputation. The topic of Professor McInerny's lecture may also have been a factor that contributed to the considerable success of tonight's event. Your attendance tonight and the many questions asked of Professor McInerny illustrate that Australian Catholics are genuinely concerned about, and interested in, the momentous developments in the Catholic Church in the United States.

---

99 Professor Ralph McInerny (1929-2010) served as a Professor of Philosophy at the University of Notre Dame, South Bend, United States.

I am undoubtedly speaking on behalf of all attendees when I say that Professor McInerny has provided us with an excellent description and analysis of certain events which recently occurred in the United States. These events are of tremendous interest and importance to all Catholics, especially Catholic academics. I was particularly interested in Professor McInerny's account of the campaign, waged by Catholic theologians, to discredit the authority of the Pope in relation to birth control and abortion. Professor McInerny described how Catholic academics, employed by prestigious Catholic universities, shielded behind the concept of academic freedom to argue that, in birth control matters, Catholics have the right to follow their consciences. However, when exercising their academic freedom, some of the participants in this debate conveniently overlooked a Papal statement in which it is clearly stipulated that, even in matters which do not involve *ex cathedra* statements by the Pope, Catholics should only follow their consciences after an intense, serious and sustained consideration of all relevant issues involved.

The American Catholic academics, whose views were discussed by the speaker tonight, may thereby have violated a salient and crucial aspect of academic freedom, namely a commitment to truth, which necessarily involves a consideration of all available and relevant material. These academics, to the extent that they passionately argued in favour of treating birth control and abortion as matters of personal choice, adopt a result-oriented approach. This approach involves a tendency on the part of these academics to interpret existing Church law to achieve a pre-ordained or preferred result. In this context, I noted Professor McInerny's point that the American press uncritically assumed that the rebellious Catholic academics were right to question the authority of the Pope. Such lack of objectivity and impartiality is also displayed regularly by many Australian journalists.

Professor McInerny described how American academics, who waged a campaign to attack the Pope's authority, developed a theory according to which the Pope, when he speaks *ex cathedra*, is restating or reaffirming what has already been accepted by the Vatican Council. This theory, as Professor McInerny explained, is based on the idea that the Pope's statements must be the result of consensus or of a democratic decision-making process. This idea leads to the subversion of the Pope's authority and results in serious, perhaps insurmountable, disciplinary problems within the Church. This was illustrated by Professor McInerny with a discussion of the story of Catholic theologian, Charles Curran, who claimed that he was targeted by the Vatican for punishment because he dissented from the Church's teaching on issues such as abortion, contraception, divorce and homosexuality.[100] In Father's Curran view, these practices may, depending on the circumstances, be morally acceptable.

In his lecture, Professor McInerny reveals the existence of one of the perennial issues in Catholic university education, namely the extent to which a Catholic university, and the unrestricted pursuit of academic freedom can coexist. Professor McInerny believes that Catholic universities should reaffirm their strong support for the ethos and values upon which these institutions are based. The claim that these institutions have the right to repudiate any claims which are incompatible with traditional Christian Catholic values is, in my opinion, eminently reasonable and could be regarded as an exercise of a University's institutional academic freedom.[101]

---

100 See David G. Savage, "Curran Says Rome Fired Him for Moderate Views", available at: https://www.latimes.com/archives/la-xpm-1986-08-21-mn-17527-story.html.
101 See about "academic freedom", Gabriël A. Moens, "Academic Freedom: An Eroded Concept?" in Gabriël A. Moens, *Academic Freedom Today*, 16 (57) Bulletin of the Australian Society of Legal Philosophy 1991/92, 57-70.

It could be said that Professor McInerny's strong support for the authority of the Pope, and the doctrine of the Pope's infallibility, find support in history. Indeed, even a perfunctory consideration of the history of the Church reveals that, during the papacy of Pope Saint Paul VI, Church discipline was significantly relaxed. Nevertheless, when Pope Saint Paul VI wrote about birth control and abortion in his Encyclical Letter, *Humanae Vitae*,[102] he used strong and unequivocal language to reaffirm what had been the law of the Church since time immemorial. He stated:

> We base Our words on the first principles of a human and Christian doctrine of marriage when We are obliged once more to declare that the direct interruption of the generative process already begun and, above all, all direct abortion, even for therapeutic reasons, are to be absolutely excluded as lawful means of regulating the number of children.

This strongly worded statement certainly indicates that the Holy Spirit steps in to preserve the purity of the Church's law and the authority of the Pope, precisely in situations where a relaxation of this law and Papal authority would have been expected.

Professor McInerny's lecture documented, in an admirable manner, the revolt of the theologians in Catholic universities in the United States. Consequently, the members of his audience became well-informed about these American developments.

We have been told by the Chairman that Professor McInerny is a keen writer of stories, especially detective stories. I will certainly become an avid and devoted reader of these stories, because if this lecture is an indication, Professor McInerny possesses the ability to discuss, in a penetrating manner, difficult moral, social, and religious issues. Allow me to say that Professor McInerny possesses

---

102 *Humanae Vitae* is dated 25 July 1968.

the logical rigour of a Hercule Poirot and the sharp intuition of a Sherlock Holmes!

We all hope that Professor McInerny will have an opportunity to return to Australia soon. As your home University, the prestigious University of Notre Dame, is sponsoring The University of Notre Dame Australia, which is now being developed as Australia's first private Catholic university, the opportunity may arise again to benefit from your thinking and wide erudition. The University of Notre Dame is not only famous for its internationally acclaimed sports team but, as we have all witnessed tonight, for the ability of at least one of its celebrated Professors, to contribute significantly to the intellectual and spiritual life of Australia's Catholic Community.

11

OUR FREE AUSTRALIAN SOCIETY
PROMISE OR REALITY?
(1994)

1. Introduction

In the past, freedom of speech has been taken for granted by most Australians. However, there has recently been an increasing number of attempts, by governments of both persuasions around Australia, to restrict the right of Australians to freely express their opinion. Even if Australians speak out on issues of concern to them, their views are sometimes ridiculed and not taken seriously by our leaders. In this paper, I propose to argue that Australia is developing into a society where governments, policymakers and trendsetters seek to impose their views on others, thereby effectively impeding the right of others to express their views with impunity from punishment.

My argument first involves a consideration of the development, by the High Court of Australia, of a right to freedom of speech in political matters.

2. Freedom of speech in political matters

In 1991, the Commonwealth Parliament adopted the *Political Broadcasts and Political Disclosures Act* which restricted electoral advertising during election periods. The legislation aimed at ensuring that the election process would not be corrupted by those who, because of their wealth, were able to buy television or broadcast time to propagate their views.

This legislation was, however, invalidated by the High Court on the ground that it infringed an implied constitutional right of freedom of communication with respect to political matters: *Australian Capital Television Pty Ltd v Commonwealth*.[103] Mason CJ argued that free speech, at least in relation to public affairs and political discussion, is necessary in order to ensure the accountability of members of Parliament. He pointed out that freedom of communication is indispensable to that accountability. In the absence of such a freedom of communication, representative government, namely government by the people through their elected representatives, would fail to achieve its purpose There are similar statements by other Justices of the High Court in this case

In my opinion, the prohibition on political advertising was a monstrous invasion of free speech. The legislative restriction went right to the heart of democratic values: it prohibited political communication, the core of free speech in a liberal democratic society. The restriction was imposed at the most important time in the political process, namely the period preceding elections. This is the time when information is most needed by voters about candidates and parties, the time when people most wish to speak. It strains credibility to assert that such a restriction might not be obnoxious in a democratic society.

---

103 177 CLR 106 (1992).

The people do not need to be shielded from political speech. They do not need to be guided as to the sorts of political messages that they may see or hear. If these messages influence the exercise of their democratic rights, it is even more important that people be able to receive them. Such paternalistic political censorship ill befits a democratic society.

Most of the justifications of the restriction were unpersuasive. Convincing evidence was at no stage offered of the link between political advertising on television and radio, and corruption or undue influence in the political process. The government might be entitled to address such a pre-existing problem, within limits, but it did not establish the existence of such a problem.

In defence of its legislation, it was argued by the Government that television advertising debases or trivialises political debate. Even if this claim is compelling, it is not enough reason for restricting political advertising. The best way of ensuring that false ideas are exposed as false is to allow them to be aired openly. As a learned American judge, Oliver Wendell Holmes observed long ago: "the ultimate good desired is better reached by free trade in ideas -- that the best test of truth is the power of thought to get itself accepted in the competition of the market."[104] If the people do not like the messages given in a political party's advertising, they may exercise their choice accordingly at the ballot box.

One of the judges in *Australian Capital Television Pty Ltd*, Brennan J, argued, however, that the restriction could be considered a legitimate restriction upon free speech. According to him, the Government's legislation was not obviously invalid because a person's right to communicate is limited by the public's interest in ensuring that political parties were not subject to corruption or undue

---

104 Abrams v United States, 250 US 616, 630 (1919).

influence by those who finance them. Brennan J said: "It was open to the Parliament to conclude, as the experience of the majority of liberal democracies has demonstrated, that representative government can survive and flourish without paid political advertising on the electronic media during election periods."[105] Of course, democracy is not going to crash if the government's legislation is declared valid. But the appropriate question is whether the prohibition was compatible with freedom of speech. That, it clearly was not.

Brennan J himself rather overestimated the corrosive effects of free speech about political matters. He fully accepted the government's claim that the legislation was passed with the object of "minimizing the risk of corruption or of reducing the untoward advantage of wealth on the formation of political opinion".[106] It is very difficult indeed to see how this statement by Brennan J in any way justifies a restriction on electoral advertising. Accepting for the sake of argument the likelihood of corruption attributable to the need for campaign donations, the target in such a case ought surely to be political donations rather than a medium of communication. In this context, it should be noted, however, that banning campaign donations would also raise substantial questions of freedom of association with respect to political matters. Even if it were accepted that the great expense of broadcast advertising is likely to create a sense of obligation on the part of political parties, it is the financial factor which is the problem rather than the speech itself. Why then did the government fail to ban political donations rather than free speech?

What is the most likely explanation for the electoral advertising restriction? There is the strong probability that the government was concerned, not with corruption but with the effect of an advertising campaign on itself – the effect of free speech. It is also

---

105   Supra n. 103, para, 21.
106   Supra n. 103, para. 12.

likely that the government considered that it could not afford to speak via the mediums concerned and was eager to deny its opponents the benefit of accessing them. The legislation was a partisan measure designed to advantage a party short of funds. In short, the government's arguments about corruption and undue influence were little more than a smokescreen.

In summary: there are enough compelling reasons as to why the advertising law was an outrageous attempt by the Federal Government to distort the political process and to interfere with the people's rights to choose their elected representatives.

3. The "public figure defence" to claims of defamation

It is common knowledge that there is a demonstrable tendency in Australia for politicians to initiate defamation proceedings against those who offend them. An important area on which the High Court has recently reserved judgment is defamation law. It is, at present, considering whether the Commonwealth Constitution requires state defamation law to recognise a "public figure defence" as in the United States.[107]

The origin of the public figure defence was the United States Supreme Court's famous 1964 decision *New York Times v Sullivan*.[108] Under the public figure defence, a politician cannot recover damages for a defamatory falsehood relating to his official conduct "unless he proves that the statement was made with 'actual malice' – that is, with knowledge that it was false or with reckless disregard of whether it was false or true."[109] The public figure defence thus protects even false statements on the ground that freedom of speech

---

[107] Note that the High Court created a new defence to defamation actions involving political figures in Theophanous v Herald & Weekly Times Ltd, 182 CLR 104 (1994) and Stephens v West Australian Newspapers Ltd, 182 CLR 211 (1994).
[108] 376. US 254 (1964).
[109] Ibid., 279-280, per Goldberg J.

needs "breathing space" in order to survive. Defamatory speech about private figures where the speech concerns some matter of "public concern" is also protected.

Even common sense suggest, that such a public figure defence to claims of defamation is highly desirable because it encourages citizens to scrutinise the activities and behaviour of elected representatives, who know or should know, that election to Parliament will inevitably invite public scrutiny of their activities.

I do not know how the High Court will deal with this issue because "the public figure defence is alien to the common law. However, in a recent British House of Lords decision upholding freedom of the press, Lord Keith of Kinkel commented that, "every citizen has a right to criticise an inefficient or corrupt government without fear of civil as well as criminal prosecution. This absolute privilege is founded on the principle that it is advantageous for the public interest that the citizens should not be in any way fettered in his statements, and where the public service or due administration of justice is involved he shall have the right to speak his mind freely."[110]

A public figure defence was no part of Australian law in 1900. It is most unlikely that the Framers of our Constitution considered such a defence necessary for the maintenance of our system of government.

4. Other legislative attacks on freedom of speech

Even though the 1992 free speech cases appear encouraging, there is a wealth of legislation and practices which impedes attempts by Australians to speak out about controversial issues.

---

[110] Derbyshire County Council v Times Newspapers Ltd and Others [1992] 1 QB 770 (CA). Aff'd [1993] AC 534; [1993] 1 All ER 1011 (HL).

For example, in 1989, New South Wales, under a Liberal Government, enacted the *Anti-Discrimination (Racial Vilification) Amendment Act*. It provides for the imposition of criminal sanctions on people whose speech incited hatred towards, serious contempt for or severe ridicule of others on the ground of race. The maximum penalty is six months imprisonment. Prosecutions are subject to the consent of the Attorney-General. This legislation is obnoxious because a person could be punished under it even if he or she did not intend to incite racial hatred. The legislation does not require that intent be proved: all that is required to be established beyond the expression that it is "threatening, abusive or insulting" is an objective likelihood that hatred will be stirred up. It overlooks that the emergence of hatred may be an indirect and completely unintended effect of the utterance and may be the product of a totally unreasonable and irrational response on the part of listeners.

A major concern is that a mere attempt to campaign for repeal of the Act could constitute a violation of it. Furthermore, the Act appears to impede advocacy of the view that the Act itself has contributed to racial hostility, through causing resentment at attacks on freedom of speech as a long-cherished part of our Australian heritage. Similar legislation is likely to be enacted by the Commonwealth and other States.[111]

A Commonwealth Racial Vilification Law will be based on international conventions, the provisions of which inhibit rights

---

[111] The Racial Discrimination Act 1975 (Cth) contains the controversial section 18C: "(1) It is unlawful for a person to do an act, otherwise than in private, if (a) the act is reasonably likely, in all the circumstances, to offend, insult, humiliate or intimidate another person or a group of people; and (b) the act is done because of the race, colour or national or ethnic origin of the other person or of some or all of the people in the group." An incisive analysis of section 18C is offered in Joshua Forrester, Lorraine Finlay and Augusto Zimmermann, *No Offence Intended: Why 18C is Wrong*, Connor Court Publishing, 2016. See also Gabriël A. Moens, "Eroding our Rights: Towards Mind Control?", *Australia and World Affairs*, No. 23, Summer 1994, 21-30.

and freedoms. For example, paragraph 2 of Article 20 of the International Covenant on Civil and Political Rights (Covenant) provides that, "Any advocacy of national, racial or religious hatred that constitutes incitement to discrimination, hostility or violence shall be prohibited by law." This prohibition is obviously overbroad and would have a profound chilling effect upon speech about controversial subjects. Indeed, such a provision could certainly be used to justify grave interferences with freedom of speech, and it could become a dangerous means of censorship of ideas unpopular with current intellectual orthodoxy. It would be possible for individuals to argue that a reluctance, on the part of the government, to prohibit such "advocacy of racial or religious hatred" constitutes a violation of the Covenant.

"Incitement" to discrimination can be a very elastic concept indeed. Paragraph 2 of Article 20 of the Covenant, if incorporated in an Australian law, could undoubtedly be used to inhibit free public debate about an extraordinary range of issues such as affirmative action, immigration, and native land title. It is unacceptable in a free society that such devices be used to limit public debate to the expression of opinions that are deemed acceptable by a cultural elite. A provision like paragraph 2 of Article 20 would look singularly unattractive in the law of a nation, like Australia, that professes its devotion to the free expression of ideas. However, other provisions of the Covenant, especially those that make the exercise of rights subject to the maintenance of "public morality" or "security" may be accepted by most people as a justified restriction on their rights.

The New South Wales legislation has recently been amended to prohibit "derogatory" comments about homosexuality. Such legislation, even if well-intended, will probably have the unintended effect of suppressing the expression of a diverse range of views related to homosexuality.

A recent American case provides a poignant example. The applicant in *Doe v University of Michigan*[112] was accused of having violated the University's Speech Code, officially known as the Policy on Discrimination and Discriminatory Harassment of Students in the University Environment. The applicant was a Psychology graduate student who specialised in the interdisciplinary study of biological bases of individual differences in personality traits and mental abilities. He argued that, "certain controversial theories positing biologically-based differences between sexes and races might be perceived as 'sexist' and 'racist' by some students, and he feared that discussion of such theories might be sanctionable under the Policy." His fears were reinforced when he was subjected to a formal hearing, provided for under the Policy, because he had expressed his belief, in the context of a social work research class, that homosexuality was a disease that could be treated psychologically.

In this context, it is fair to mention that in Australia there is a fear of censure by the Human Rights Committee of the United Nations. Australia has permitted the Committee to hear complaints from individuals of violations of the International Covenant under its First Optional Protocol.[113] The Covenant is certainly of concern to Australian courts and is frequently referred to by the judges these days.[114] This Covenant was recently in the news when the Committee held that Tasmanian laws, which prohibit the practice of homosexuality in public, violate the Covenant.

---

112   721 F.Supp. 852 (E.D. Mich. 1989).
113   999 UNTS 302 (1966).
114   See especially Mabo v Queensland (No. 2), 175 CLR 1 (1992) at 42 (Brennan J). See also Dietrich v R, 177 CLR 292 (1992) at 391-293 (Mason CJ and McHugh J, actually using the words "potential censure" at 391; 404 (Brennan J), 416-417 (Deane J), 424-426 (Dawson J), 434-435 (Toohey J), 444 (Gaudron J).

Another recent example of the influence of international conventions, even if these Conventions do reflect the will of the people, is the *Industrial Relations Reform Act* 1994 (Cth). This legislation was adopted by the Federal Parliament, using the external affairs power. This power enables the Parliament to implement international conventions that impose certain obligations on Australia. It is regrettable that the Act was never properly debated in Parliament. Important and far-reaching reforms should not be adopted without sustained argument. The legislation makes it difficult for an employer to sack an incompetent or inefficient worker. An employer who wishes to sack an incompetent employee will have to go through an expensive and difficult procedure. This will inevitably increase the cost of employing a person. The legislation is based on Conventions, the terms of which are now enshrined in the Australian Act. For example, the legislation provides for minimum entitlements of employees, thereby giving effect to the International Labor Organization (ILO) Minimum Wage Fixing Convention.[115] The limitation on an employer's ability to terminate employment gives effect to the Termination of Employment Convention.[116] The Industrial Relations Commission must take account of the Workers with Family Responsibilities Convention[117] in performing its duties of conciliation and arbitration. My point is that increasing federal power by use of the external affairs power, which involves the arrogation by the Federal Parliament to itself of the right to make laws with regard to the subject matter of international conventions, implicitly removes the rights of people to determine their own destiny – a serious matter by any standard.

When the electoral advertising case was decided, the High Court also considered a Commonwealth law which made it an offence

---

115 ILO Convention, 1970 (No. 131).
116 ILO Convention, 1982 (No. 158).
117 ILO Convention, 1981 (No. 156).

to publish material calculated to bring the Industrial Relations Commission into disrepute. The law made it an offence to criticise a governmental institution, the members of which were responsible for regulating industrial relations in this country! Like in the advertising case, a majority on the High Court declared the legislation invalid on the basis that it infringed an implied right to freedom in relation to public affairs: *Nationwide News v Wills*.[118]

5. The importance of a federal system

It is obvious that the reliance placed in Australia on international conventions strengthens the central government at the expense of state governments. This is an important insight because we should not, in my opinion, underestimate the protection of rights that is offered by the functioning of a healthy federal system. This has been observed even in the United States where the Supreme Court has only recently stated that state sovereignty is not merely an end but exists for the protection of individuals. Federalism implicitly protects individuals because it prevents an excessive accumulation of power in either level of government. Where there is an adequately functioning balance of power between the States and the federal governments, the possibility of arbitrary governance by either level of government is greatly reduced.

In Australia, governmental power is divided among numerous governments, each of limited powers. Furthermore, the party holding most seats in the federal and state Lower Houses seldom dominates the Upper House. These institutional factors are powerful limitations upon arbitrary government.

Overreaching by the Commonwealth is likely to be challenged by

---

118   177 CLR 1 (1992).

the States. Overreaching by the States in the suppression of citizens' rights is likely to be remedied by paramount Commonwealth legislation. The electoral advertising case provides an instructive example of how a division of powers between the federal and state governments protect rights. As mentioned before, in that case, the High Court invalidated the Commonwealth government's prohibition upon electoral advertising on the ground that it violated an implied constitutional right of freedom of communication regarding the government of the Commonwealth. The relevant Commonwealth law was successfully challenged by the New South Wales State government. Thus, the invalidation of the political advertising restriction is the result of federalism working properly in Australia. A former Chief Justice, Sir Harry Talbot Gibbs. clearly expressed the benefits of federalism when he said that, "the most effective way to curb political power is to divide it. A Federal Constitution, which brings about a division of power in actual practice, is a more secure protection for basic political freedoms than a bill of rights."[119]

6. Imposition of the preferred views of policymakers and trendsetters

I have thus far mainly concentrated on recent legislation which, in my opinion, adversely affects freedom of speech. In addition, there are many documented attempts by present policymakers and trendsetters to impose their views on others who dare to present an alternative, but less trendy, view. This imposition takes several forms.

First, people who avail themselves of their right to contribute to

---

[119] Sir Harry Gibbs, "A Constitutional Bill of Rights", in K. Baker (ed.), An Australian Bill of Rights: Pro and Contra, Melbourne, Institute of Public Affairs, 1986, 325.

public affairs are sometimes humiliated. Humiliation often has the effect of subjecting them to severe ridicule. For example, most people would be aware that at the time of the last election there was quite a bit of discussion about the proposed reduction of tariffs which would have directly and seriously affected the sugar industry. A reduction in the tariff would, in effect, have made the Australian product uncompetitive, leading to unemployment and, in some cases, even destitution. I am not making a judgment about the wisdom of reducing tariffs in cases where it would demonstrably lead to serious hardship. Instead, I deplore the arrogance of politicians, some of whom were reported as having made derogatory comments about sugar cane farmers. For example, it was reported that a politician had said that the government need not be concerned about a possible backlash because "these sugar cane farmers would not know which day of the week it was." This is an important, yet not an isolated, example of the contempt in which people are held by some politicians whose actions indicate that, in their view, people are voiceless and unable to make decisions for themselves.

Second, policymakers impose their preferred policies and views on people by encouraging members of minorities to complain about mainstream Australians. To paraphrase George Orwell: "we are all equal, but some are more equal than others." In Australia, an ever-increasing number of human rights practitioners encourage the making of complaints against people who dare to speak out against the prevailing orthodoxy. Let me give you an example of this trend. The Queensland Anti-Discrimination Commissioner has recently been quoted as saying: "I think the fact that we don't yet have a large number of complaints from Aboriginal people is a signal that we are still not quite reaching them to tell them about their rights and the services available to them." She believes that governments have the God-given right to change the behaviour of people. She stated: "I think it is a period of great social change and at the forefront of this is our work and observing how legislation and government can influence and lead to behaviour change." She also went on to say that, "Because most judges are male there's no question at all that they obviously have limited experience of a woman's view and experience of particular situations, especially in cases of domestic violence." A society that encourages the making of frivolous complaints is a society that inevitably ends up censoring speech.

Third, policymakers constantly assume uncritically that they know what is best for the people of this country, rather than letting the people speak for themselves. For example, there is the relentless push by some government forces to reserve 50% of parliamentary seats for women. What I do not understand is that these pronouncements are made without considering whether women in fact do want these changes. It is a change which is government-driven rather than accepted or pursued voluntarily by women in general.

I have, for many years now, collected examples of the practices which some so-called enlightened people seriously put forward in the name of affirmative action. For example, many university advertisements specify that women are underrepresented in the Academy and that, therefore, female applicants are encouraged to apply. It surprises me that under such a system, there are still men who are willing to apply for positions which may well have been earmarked for women only. Some universities are considering women-only promotion rounds, excluding men, thereby violating the most basic principle upon which all affirmative action legislation is presumably based, namely that positions will go to the most meritorious applicant.

7. Vision of an ideal society

I now propose, by way of conclusion, to describe my vision of an ideal society. Such a society is a society where there is genuine freedom of choice and where those who are indisputably in need of help are given government assistance. It is a society which adheres to the principle that the people themselves, as opposed to the government, know what is best for them. My ideal society is a society where governments only interfere with people's lives when necessary to prevent serious harm to others. It is also a society where there is no attempt by governments or lobby groups to sanitise the expression of people who disagree with them.

The establishment of such a society will be a difficult, perhaps impossible, task. Most of our newspapers have progressivist, socialist leanings. A few weeks ago, when Tony Abbott and Bronwyn Bishop were elected to the House of Representatives, the Sydney Morning Herald severely criticised the Liberal Party for having preselected these two candidates. They were described as conservatives, who are completely out of touch with the people and whose major deficiency lies in their inability to embrace modern progressivist ideas. According to the writer of the newspaper article, people are entitled to have as their representatives, people who assiduously and aggressively pursue progressive policies! Conservatives are non-persons!

What we need in Australia are strong political leaders. I am not convinced that we have the conservative leadership capable of confronting the present Labor Government. In this context, I have heard it said on numerous occasions by Coalition politicians that there are no longer pronounced ideological differences between the Coalition and the Labor Party. Nevertheless, the Coalition wants us to vote for them because they claim to be "better" economic managers. Such reason results in political suicide because, in the absence of ideological differences between the two main political protagonists, voters do not have compelling reasons to vote for the Coalition. This is so because whether a Party is a better or worse economic manager would exclusively depend upon the politicians who, at any given time, are involved in these Parties. Thus, if Labor has better candidates, conservative voters will have good reasons to vote for Labor. In such a system, a choice would no longer be dependent on ideology.

My ideal society is a society where the people should be given a chance to look after their own interests, rather than having these interests determined by governments. The best government is the government that governs least.[120] This will only be possible if the size of the elaborate welfare state, which has been created during the last decades, even with the help of the Coalition, is substantially reduced. Government largesse creates dependency on the government. This has the unusual result that, even in times of high unemployment, it is possible for a Labor Government to be re-elected to office. Indeed, the unemployed receive generous government handouts, which make them vote for their benefactor – the all-powerful Big Brother. The welfare state, in turn, creates and fosters the establishment of mighty bureaucracies, the members of which can hardly be restrained by law. Such a system is fundamentally opposed to a desire, among people, to take the future in their own hands, without being unnecessarily restrained by Big Brother. I think it is time to speak up!

---

120   Henry David Thoreau, Resistance to Civil Government, para. 1.

12

HOW TO MISMANAGE ORGANISATIONS
(2014)

1. Introduction

In an editorial, published in *Leader*, the official Journal of the Australian Institute of Management (WA), Professor Gary Martin writes that, "Organisations across the corporate, government, not-for-profit and charitable sectors are flooding our workplaces with incompetent bosses by persisting in promoting people to management roles without due regard to the attributes required for management success."[121] This statement reminded me of an article I had written in 2014 in which I discuss the same phenomenon. The paper was hugely popular and has been read avidly around the world. In this Collection, I propose to provide my readership with an updated, but shortened, version of this paper.

It is not unusual for employees to allege that the organisations for which they work are mismanaged. Even if these allegations

---

[121] Gary Martin, "It's official: Empty suits make the worst kind of bosses", *Leader*, No. 18, March 2020, 4.

are unsupported, the fact that they are raised regularly justifies an examination of how organisations may be mismanaged. During my career as a university academic and manager, and in other management roles, I have observed and experienced noted examples of mismanagement. Although my observations are largely based on my own knowledge and experience as an academic, they are supported by scholarly and empirical management research and informed by comparative analysis. The fact that I have worked in several non-academic organisations, including chambers of commerce, arbitration institutions, law firms and media organisations, has provided me with the opportunity to compare different management approaches and styles.

This paper concentrates on three practices which, in my opinion, constitute 'mismanagement': (a) the appointment of employees to their level of incompetence, which in turn may lead to occupational stress and low staff morale, (b) the appointment of employees who are deemed to be less "intelligent" than, or "inferior" to, the appointers, (c) the centralisation of resources which involves restructuring and associated change management. I will argue that these three mismanagement practices are pervasive and misconceived. However, the actions which might result in the mismanagement of organisations are infinite and most employees would undoubtedly be able to supply examples of other odious management practices.

2. The appointment of employees to their level of incompetence: The Peter Principle

A practice by senior management which may potentially result in the mismanagement of their organisations involves the appointment of employees to their level of incompetence which, in turn, may lead to occupational stress and low staff morale.

In their celebrated book *The Peter Principle*, Laurence J. Peter and Raymond Hull argue that, "in a hierarchy every employee tends to rise to his level of incompetence."[122] There is evidence suggesting that occupational stress and low staff morale are generated or exacerbated if there is a systemic tendency to promote people to positions for which they are not properly prepared or for which their qualifications and experience are inadequate.

The Peter Principle is based upon the assumption that appointment of an employee to a higher-level position is a reward for excellence at the lower level. The appointee's incompetence usually only reveals itself after the employee has assumed the higher-level position. Professor Martin provides an instructive example: a successful salesperson may be promoted to the position of sales manager, and removed from the day-to-day sales activity, because of their ability to regularly exceed the sales target of the company. Also, the salesperson may be promoted with the intention that they will teach their sales techniques to the sales staff, thereby boosting their performance. However, if the employee is promoted to their level of incompetence, the company may be forfeiting the income that otherwise would be generated by the excellent salesperson. He makes the following observation:

> While it might seem logical to choose the most talented salesperson to be the team's new sales manager, that thinking is fundamentally flawed – the job of an individual sales professional is substantially different to that of a leader of a team of salespeople. The sales manager's job might well require product knowledge along with sales kills. More importantly, it

---

[122] Laurence J Peter Laurence and Raymond Hull, *The Peter Principle*, Bantam, New York, 1972, 7. The Peter Principle was further developed in Laurence J Peter, The Peter Prescription: How to Make Things Go Right, Bantam, New York, 1973, and Laurence J Peter, Why Things Go Wrong or the Peter Principle Revisited, New York, William Morrow and Company, Inc., 1985.

will also demand an additional and substantially different set of skills to support the success of those in the team – the skills of management. The new sales manager is unlikely to know how to be a good manager and might even lack the passion for leading others. In that case, the net result is the workplace loses an outstanding salesperson and gains a poor manager.[123]

Moreover, if the sales manager does not function effectively in their new management role, they may generate a stressful environment that infects the whole company. Common sense suggests, and experience confirms, that an ability to exceed the sales target is a poor indicator as to how well an appointee will do at the senior management level. Specifically, it does not usually reveal the salesperson's capacity to manage staff.

Another example, which is not uncommon in universities, is to appoint capable researchers or teachers to senior management roles, even the Vice- Chancellor's or President's role. Indeed, even a perfunctory review of the Higher Education Supplement of *The Australian* reveals that the Australian university landscape is blighted by senior managers who, for a number of reasons, including a sense of self-importance, overstated confidence and/or arrogance or an inability to use "power" wisely, are ultimately costly failures, even though they may have excelled in their previous roles.

The Peter Principle, although it is predominantly used to explain bad management decisions, is only an expression of a more general principle, namely that there is a tendency in society's endeavours for people to be pushed to their level of incompetence. For example, in an educational context, this principle can even be used for the purpose of evaluating preferential admission programmes in professional schools. These programmes, which commonly exist in universities in the United States, aim at increasing minority

---

123   Supra n. 121, 4-5.

enrolment in professional schools. However, such a programme can be criticised on the ground that there can be no adequate numerical increase because it only pushes minority students from lesser to better schools, namely schools with more demanding admission standards.[124] This phenomenon, which is known as the "moving-up phenomenon", illustrates that each school, by its preferential admission, simply takes minority students away from other schools whose admission standards are further down the scale. Any net gain in the total number of minority students admitted must come, if it comes at all, from those schools the admission standards of which are at the bottom of the scale and take students whom they would not otherwise have admitted. Hence, in this context, the implementation of the Peter Principle, as a more generalised principle which is not limited to the management of organisations, causes large numbers of minority students to attend schools the admission standards of which they do not meet, instead of attending other schools the normal standards of which they do meet.[125]

The Peter Principle does not indicate how an appointee to a position which exceeds their level of competence, could be removed from that position. Good management requires the development of pathways to enable people to be returned to their level of competence without substantial loss of face. In an interesting article, Carly Chynoweth provides examples of Chief Executive Officers who voluntarily relinquished their positions to return to their previously held deputy position. She argues that

---

[124] Gabriël A. Moens, "Preferential Admission Programs in Professional Schools: Defunis, Bakke, and Grutter", 48 *Loyola Law Review*, 2002, 411-503, 470-477; Martin H Redish, "Preferential Law School Admissions and he Equal Protection Clause: An Analysis of the Competing Arguments", 22 *University of California Los Angeles Law Review*, 1974, 343-400, 393-394.

[125] Clyde W. Summers, "Preferential Admissions: An Unreal Solution to a Real Problem", 2 *University of Toledo Law Review*, 1970, 377-402, 384.

this is not a retrograde step and does not constitute failure because there is a skill to lead from behind the curtain, certainly if this is more suited to the skills and goals of the relevant employee.[126] However, in most cases the removal of incompetent employees who do not voluntarily return to their level of competence may be administratively very difficult or prohibitively expensive. This is because the existence of numerous legal impediments and institutional procedural safeguards may prevent or complicate the removal of those who do not function effectively at the higher level.

Several matters are not considered by the Peter Principle. The Peter Principle does not concern itself with the question as to why a capable and competent person may fail to advance in a hierarchical structure. Failure to advance in a hierarchical structure may be caused by the inability or unwillingness of management to recognise the assumed or perceived potential of an employee. This failure may be caused by jealousy or by the employee's lack of ambition, or by managers who have been promoted to their level of incompetence. Sometimes, persons in their early careers do not function optimally because they have not yet been able to marshal their potential talents. For example, young university teachers may not be the "best" possible teachers they can be because of their lack of experience or confidence. However, they may later achieve excellent results once their potential is realised by working diligently, developing maturity, and even exploiting luck and opportunities. The Peter Principle also does not deal with the interesting phenomenon, recognised by Roderick Swaab, that too much talent on a team often means that a team "performs worse overall"[127] and hence, a tipping point can be reached where decline

---

126 Carly Chynoweth, "Be the power behind the throne", *The Sunday Times*, 6 July 2014, Section 7, 2.
127 Carly Chynoweth, "Too much talent kills team spirit", *The Sunday Times*, 6 July 2014, Section 7, 3.

sets in.

Instead, the Peter Principle explains why employees, who perform capably at a lower level, do not perform at a higher level. Essentially, these employees cannot "grow" into their allocated task but have nevertheless been appointed to perform it. Thus, the Peter Principle applies to a situation where employees are inherently unable to perform their job because of their *incompetence*, which in turn, is generated by mismatching appointees' qualifications, skills and experience, and the demands of the employee's occupational role. This mismatching constitutes a stressor, which causes occupational or role-related stress which is "an adaptive response to a situation that is perceived as challenging or threatening to the person's well-being."[128]

3. The Peter Principle and the Management of Stress

The professional literature regarding stress management deals extensively with the causes of stress, known as "stressors".[129] Stressors include, but are not limited to, interpersonal, organisational, physical, environmental, and occupational factors.

The proposition that occupational stress may be caused by a mismatch of the professional role of employees, and their qualifications and experience, is instinctively perceived as valid. This is because employees are not expected to perform their tasks competently if their qualifications, skills, and experience do not properly prepare them for the challenges of their professional role. This point is illustrated by McShane & Travaglione who refer to a

---

[128] Steven McShane and Tony Travaglione, *Organisational Behaviour on the Pacific Rim*, 2nd ed., North Ryde, McGraw-Hill Irwin, 2007, 202.
[129] Alix Needham, *The Stress Management Book*, East Roseville, NSW, Simon & Schuster Australia, 1996, 8-17; McShane and Travaglione, supra n. 128, 204-209.

report produced by the New South Wales Law Society according to which more than half of the 1800 lawyers polled had been bullied or intimidated by clients. This bullying and intimidation caused severe occupational stress, which substantially decreased these lawyers' ability to function effectively in the legal profession.[130] The situation described by these authors may occur, for example, if a successful black-letter lawyer, who performs brilliantly as a legal researcher in a law firm, is required to deal face-to-face with clients. The lawyer may be singularly deficient in their dealings with clients due to a lack of confidence, an inability to relate to people whose level of education may be minimal, or a failure to understand the "end game" or the result a client hopes to achieve when engaging a lawyer. Ultimately, the stress experienced by these lawyers could be characterised as occupational stress which is caused by their inability to communicate effectively with their clients. Indeed, the realisation that a mismatching of a person's professional role and their qualifications, skills and experience may result in occupational or role-related stress has spawned an industry which aims at neutralising the deleterious effect of the Peter Principle in operation.

A review of the relevant literature also reveals that authors, in general, regard a limited amount of stress as necessary for the achievement of an employee's goals.[131] As Stone argues, "When there is no stress, job challenges are non-existent."[132] Similarly, John Message confidently states that, "Stress is a powerful servant but a tyrannical master. It can be a rich source of energy in the service of achievement and creativity; or it can be a source of corrosion

---

130   Supra n. 128, 205.
131   Peter Hanson, *The Joy of Stress*, Sydney, Pan Books, 1986, 15-19.
132   Raymond J. Stone, *Human Resource Management*, 3rd ed., Brisbane, John Wiley & Sons, 1995, 670.

and exhaustion."¹³³ Hence, from a management point of view, it is necessary to ascertain at which point stress is likely to adversely affect an employee's ability "to feel a sense of achievement and to get satisfaction from the job."¹³⁴ Occupational stress may thus have a positive effect and may even serve as a motivating force when employees' qualifications and experience match their occupational role, thereby enabling them to reach their potential. However, if a mismatch generates occupational stress, the consequences for the affected employee and the employer may be serious. The adverse effects of the application of the Peter Principle, especially the consequences of appointment to one's level of incompetence, can only be minimised by transferring employees "to jobs that better fit their competencies and values."¹³⁵

The literature also focuses on the impact of stress on managerial style, including the use by managers of their cognitive resources under stress. For example, Neil McAdam addresses the issue as to whether "stressful circumstances prompt a reversion to earlier less mature cognitive and expressive repertoires in the individual's attempt to manage the pressures of the noxious environment."¹³⁶ McAdam's observation, in effect, deals with the role played by "emotional intelligence" to confront and resolve problems generated by incompetent management.

Peter Salovey and John D. Mayer have described "emotional intelligence" as the "ability to monitor one's own and others' feelings and emotions, to discriminate among them and to use this

---

133   John Message, *A Practical Guide to Stress and Its Management*, Hutchinson of Australia, 1986, 6.
134   Supra n. 132, 671.
135   Supra n. 128, 216.
136   Neil McAdam, "Situational Stress and Restriction of Stylistic Repertoire in High Potential Managerial Aspirants: Implications for the Implementation of the 'New Organization'", 12(1) *Journal of Management and Organization*, 2006, 40-67, 48.

information to guide one's thinking and actions."[137] They point out that, "The emotionally intelligent person ... attends to emotion in the path toward growth. Emotional intelligence involves self-regulation appreciative of the fact that temporarily hurt feelings or emotional restraint is often necessary in the service of a greater objective."[138]

Many readers of this paper would probably be able to recall circumstances at work where high levels of stress were generated by people who were not able to control their emotions and, consequently, contributed to an explosive situation. This often involves screaming and yelling, the levelling of accusations (often in public) or the sending of obnoxious e-mail messages which make for horrifying reading. Thus, "emotional intelligence" is related directly to the performance by managers of their duties. A lack of emotional intelligence is a cause of mismanagement of organisations and, at the same time, a manifestation of managerial incompetence which, in turn, may have been instigated by the implementation of the Peter Principle.

4. The appointment of employees who are deemed to be less "intelligent" than, or "inferior" to, the appointers

The robustness of an organisation could easily be eroded if senior management were to appoint employees, who are deemed to be less "intelligent" than, or "inferior" to, the appointers. This is a common occurrence in most organisations, and in my experience, is especially prevalent in universities. As a member of selection committees, I have often been appalled at the elimination of applicants whom I regarded as promising and enthusiastic. Instead,

---

[137] Peter Salovey and John D. Mayer, "Emotional Intelligence", 9(3) *Imagination, Cognition, and Personality*, 1990, 185-213, 189.
[138] Ibid., 201.

these committees often appointed applicants who, by all standards, would be unimaginative and ineffective and lack entrepreneurial flair, but would always be compliant, and would slavishly attempt to implement the directives of senior management. Of course, this outcome may well be dependent upon the requirements for the role, and it should be recognised that members of a selection committee could legitimately disagree on the qualifications and skills needed for the successful performance of a professional role.

The practice to appoint inferior people may be explained by the fear of senior managers of being challenged by junior employees who are more intelligent, more driven, and more entrepreneurial than them. It is not unusual for ambitious junior managers to exhibit a willingness and ability to take initiative; this is sometimes looked upon with hostility by their senior colleagues. Nevertheless, good management surely requires members of selection committees to always attempt to appoint people who are "better" than themselves. This is so for several reasons. First, the relevant organisation presumably would run better if the most competent persons were to be appointed to staff positions. Second, the appointment of the most competent person to a position would also enhance the position of the appointers because they would be able to claim, quite justifiably, that (a) they have the ability to match peoples' qualifications with occupational roles, and (b) are able to manage an organisation which runs smoothly.

In this context, it is also important to emphasise that senior managers should always give credit to junior colleagues whose job-related achievements have enhanced the reputation of their organisations. Indeed, it is an inexcusable, but common, mistake for senior managers to arrogate to themselves the achievements of their junior colleagues without giving appropriate credit to those who engineered these achievements. Indeed, the failure by senior management to acknowledge the achievements of their employees leads to low staff morale and distrust between senior managers and their junior colleagues.

There have been notable attempts to ensure that jobs and competences are linked. This linkage is required either by legislation or by an organisation's legislation/regulations, or by the enterprise bargaining agreement (EBA) rules which require positions to be advertised. However, my experience suggests, that, if positions are advertised, you often get the person you do not want. Admittedly, this is an anecdotal argument; nevertheless, this outcome may, at times, be a consequence of the involvement in the appointment process of the organisation's Human Resources and Equity Committees which have little knowledge of, or appreciation for, the skills which are sought in an appointee. In many cases, these committees are merely interested in ensuring that procedural safeguards are respected, and processes followed, or that the organisation's workforce statistically reflects the total numerical strength of all groups in society. In such circumstances, the appointee is almost always a compromise appointment and may not be the "best" or most "suitable" person for the job.

5. The centralisation of resources of the organisation involving restructuring and associated change management

Centralisation "means that formal decision-making authority is held by a small group of people, typically those at the top of the organisational hierarchy."[139] Senior managers sometimes think that centralising all relevant administrative resources and services as well as concentrating decision-making in few hands, will facilitate the management of their organisations and will result in better oversight, administrative convenience, and costs-savings, by avoiding duplication.

---

139   *Supra* n. 128, 451.

However, in doing so, they overlook the costs associated with centralisation, especially non-monetary costs, such as a deterioration in staff morale. This may happen because centralisation of resources, services and decision-making typically deprives staff members of the means to control their own professional destiny and inhibits their willingness to take initiative.

The administration of an organisation's units is made more difficult because centralisation involves the removal of administrative staff members from their previously decentralised habitat and places them in a central office where they are part of a common pool of service providers. Hence, the administration officer allocated to serve a unit of the organisation often would not know the people they are working with and would be emotionally removed from, or perhaps even be disinterested in, that unit. Consequently, there is a spectacular disconnect between the administrator and those who are administered.

In this context, I have heard it said that centralised bureaucracies exist to ensure that people are prevented from doing their jobs! This is well known in a university environment, where the cumbersome and extensive research and administrative bureaucracies consist of people who impose a multitude of administrative requirements upon academics, such as numerous form-filling and reporting obligations. Such bureaucratic requirements inhibit academics from doing the research they are expected to undertake.

Employees would also be familiar with the pompous desire of an organisation's officials and central committees to develop new policies on every conceivable topic. This desire often manifests itself in an unending process the purpose of which is to develop the "best" possible policy with regards to a particular topic. Indeed, it is not unusual for organisations to have a policy on the development of policies! Committees spend much time and effort developing the best possible policy they can develop, a kind of Rolls Royce policy which encapsulates the best practice from around the world. However, once this Rolls Royce policy is adopted, the policy may well be treated with benign neglect by the organisation's community or very few resources are allocated to its implementation and monitoring, leading to a failure to achieve the desired results. The committees which draft these policies do not seem to understand that the implementation of their new policies typically increases the burdens placed upon staff members who are deemed to possess an infinite appetite for absorbing new policies. Perhaps there should be a policy on the removal of policies? Some governments have done this by introducing "one-in, one-out" rules for departments proposing new regulatory regimes.

A policy of centralisation, which is embraced by those who oppose delegation of functions, is essentially a manifestation of micro-management.[140] It is based on the assumption that only senior management can be trusted and that an organisation's survival is dependent on central decision-making. This management style stifles innovation and creates low staff morale within organisations. Sometimes, there is a never-ending pursuit of restructuring, followed by change management. Indeed, the centralisation of resources and services is often the declared aim of major restructuring projects and change management programmes, often spearheaded by a change management consultancy, costing millions of dollars and requiring an enormous amount of time and commitment, especially on the part of senior employees. In my experience, leaders, who have been promoted to their level of incompetence appear to believe that, to make an

---

140 See generally: Harry Chambers, *My Way or the Highway: The Micromanagement Survival Guide*, San Francisco, Berrett Kohler Publishers, 2004.

impact, they need to restructure their workplaces. Of course, this type of restructuring often results in centralising power into the hands of a few senior managers. Also, such practice does not empower staff members to excel in their professional activities, to enhance the reputation of their units and to maintain their viability.

These restructurings, followed by change management programmes, are very costly, not just in terms of their development and implementation, but also because there is usually also an enormous opportunity cost since employees' involvement in change management processes inevitably impacts upon the real function of organisations. There is no doubt that change management overload exists, and that people tire of constant change, especially if senior management practice micro-management and reach into areas which traditionally come within the domain of more junior members of staff.

In a centralised system, little of substance can be done without applying to various committees that inevitably take a long time to make a relevant decision. In such a system, the best operators may well be those who courageously undertake the work that needs to be done before they officially ask for permission to proceed. Once the work is successfully completed, they would then ask for permission to undertake what had already been accomplished.

6. Concluding comment

This paper has described examples of how an organisation could be mismanaged. In concentrating on three practices which, in my opinion, will result in mismanagement, I sought to indicate what managers should *not* do to reduce the mismanagement of their organisations. To successfully manage an organisation, it is important for senior management to support their organisations' employees, ensuring there are opportunities for their self-enhancement, coupled with a realisation that they need to take responsibility for their own actions. This requires the adoption of sound management practices and the pursuit of excellence.

13

THE CONTRIBUTION OF "THE CHRISTIAN FOUNDATIONS OF THE COMMON LAW" TO ENDURING IDEAS
(2018)

1. Introducing and Launching "The Christian Foundations of the Common Law"

I am delighted to have been asked to say a few words about this excellent book, *Christian Foundations of the Common Law* (Volume III: Australia) written by Professor Augusto Zimmermann.[141] My delight stems from the fact that this book contributes to a better understanding and appreciation of the Christian foundations of the Australian common law system which has served this country well for more than two centuries. Also, it is always satisfying to read a book as erudite as this one which provides an accurate and readable account of the philosophical and religious traditions which have shaped this country, which is the envy of the world

---

141 Augusto Zimmermann, *Christian Foundations of the Common Law (Volume III: Australia)*, Connor Court Publishing, 2018.

It is unusual for anyone today to write a book about this topic because we have largely lost our ability or willingness to recognise the importance of Christian values and traditions to our legal system. This is because Australia has become a predominantly secular country. There is no doubt that, these days, it needs courage to write about this topic in our increasingly secular world dominated by political correctness and progressive ideologies, which like a cancer, have invaded our way of life.

Professor Zimmermann's book is a *tour de force* for at least three reasons First, it neatly identifies the Christian foundations, values, and traditions of Australian common law. The book discusses the relevant views and contributions made by philosophers and lawyers to our common law system in an engaging and interesting manner. In this regard, it is as much a detailed historical account of the history of the common law as well as a scholarly treatment of the philosophical and religious influences of these traditions on the common law. Second, it is an immensely erudite book, replete with sophistication and information which reveals the author's deep knowledge and understanding of the Christian foundations of the common law. Third, the book reminds us that these values and traditions, which we cherish, are seriously threatened today. Indeed, the foundational values and traditions of this country are being eroded, dismantled, and in any event, seriously questioned and attacked. Everything has changed in the last twenty years or so. These changes have affected our lives, from cradle to grave. These changes include, and relate to, how and when we are born, how marriage is defined and extending to the way in which and when we die.

In our universities and intellectual circles, there is hardly any discussion of the Christian, historical and philosophical foundations of the common law. These institutions routinely and aggressively promote secular ideas and ideologies as the only acceptable views. In law schools, the teaching of legal philosophy and history is practically non-existent. Hence, we are creating a generation of lawyers who are largely ignorant of the Christian heritage of our common law. Moreover, there appears to be a determined effort to smear these traditions. Indeed, whatever was taken for granted until recently, and deemed necessary for a happy and satisfying life, is severely questioned by our present policymakers, legislators, and trendsetters. I would like to give you a few examples.

There is an unquestioned belief in science and in the ability of people to explain everything in a scientific way, leaving no room anymore for faith.[142] This approach, of course, is a tragic mistake because the more we know, the more mysteries and unexplained phenomena surface which are not amenable to scientific analysis. Hence, there will always be room for, and a need of, faith. However, scientific developments have now made it possible to manipulate the gender of our children, and cloning technology already exists. We have witnessed the adoption of same sex marriage as a legal institution in this country.[143] And increasingly, legislators around Australia promote euthanasia to enable people to determine how and when they die.[144]

Australia has taken the concept of equality, which has become the

---

142 In this context, Article 1, *The Humanist Manifesto II*, 1973 states that, "We believe ... that traditional dogmatic or authoritarian religions that place revelation, God, ritual, or creed above human needs and experience do a disservice to the human species. Any account of nature should pass the tests of scientific evidence; in our judgment, the dogmas and myths of traditional religions do not do so."
143 Marriage Amendment (Definition and Religious Freedoms) Act 2017 (Cth). This law came into effect on 9 December 2017.
144 The *Voluntary Assisted Dying Act* 2017 (Victoria) came into effect on 19 June 2019. The *Voluntary Assisted Dying Act* 2019 (Western Australia) passed the Western Australian Parliament on 10 December 2019 and received Royal Assent on 19 December 2019. It is expected to come into effect in mid-2021.

dominant value in an increasingly secular society, to its illogical extreme. There are now demands for strong affirmative action and the imposition of quotas to ensure that people are represented in positions of power and influence in accordance with their total numerical strength in society.[145] The successful same sex marriage campaign has further isolated people of faith who have opposing views, even if they are religiously inspired or mandated. This has resulted in striking consequences for free speech in that people of faith feel restrained to discuss controversial and topical issues in the public forum, especially if their views do not conform with those of policymakers and the intellectual elite. Specifically, those who rely on the right to religious freedom to offer opinions on recently adopted social engineering changes are often threatened with legal consequences if they promote their religiously inspired views. Clearly, the right to the free exercise of religion and the right to free speech are intertwined; a claim that the right to free speech has been infringed could easily be converted into a claim that freedom of religion has been violated.

As reported, so impressively, by Professor Zimmermann, the process of denigration is also happening in our institutions of higher learning. He wrote in *The Australian* that these institutions "are no longer bastions of academic freedom and excellence. It is impossible to think that academic inquiry can flourish where the intellectual apparatuses dominating these universities is built for intellectual repression and not for academic inquiry. This form of ideological imperialism has no place in an open and democratic society."

Recently, a new battleground has formed: it aims to eliminate or remove the existing exemptions in the Anti-Discrimination Act

---

[145] On Affirmative Action, see Gabriël Moens, *Affirmative Action: The New Discrimination*, The Centre for Independent Studies, 1985.

for religious schools which, at present, are still able to appoint staff, and to admit students, whose views are compatible with the religious tenets of the school.

The Prime Minister is considering the adoption of a freedom of religion Act. However, I am not certain this is the way forward because the legislation is clearly based on the idea that freedom of religion is the gift of government. Consequently, such gift could easily be taken away by subsequent governments. Moreover, the Prime Minister has also announced that he will legislate to make it illegal for schools to prohibit the dismissal of students and staff on grounds of their sexuality, thereby eliminating the exemptions that these schools currently enjoy. We are placing ourselves so much in the hands of the law and at the discretion of legislators and policymakers. We are disregarding the advice given by an American Judge, Billings Learned Hand, who reminded us long ago, that "Liberty lies in the hearts of men and women; when it dies there, no constitution, no law, no court can save it"[146], hence rights will only be adequately protected if they are nurtured in the hearts of people.

In my brief comments today, I would like to concentrate on the right to religious freedom which is certainly one of the rights that is threatened by the anti-discrimination industry and is a central theme of Professor Zimmermann's book.

2. Relevant international conventions regarding religion

There is a plethora of international human rights documents that protect the right to freely exercise one's religion in public and private. They are an attempt to codify natural rights to freedom of

---

146 Billings Learned Hand; Speech *The Spirit of Liberty* at "I am an American Day", Central Park, New York, 21 May 1944.

religion. Specifically, I refer to:

> Article 18, Universal Declaration of Human Rights
>
> *Everyone has the right to freedom of thought, conscience and religion; this right includes freedom to change his religion or belief, and freedom, either alone or in community with others and in public or private, to manifest his religious belief in teaching, practice, worship and observance.*

The Universal Declaration of Human Rights was adopted by the United Nations on 10 December 1948. It should be stressed that Article 18 provides that the right to freedom of religion includes not only freedom of religious belief, but also the right to manifest one's religious belief in public and in private. Thus, Article 18 protects religious belief and religious practice, which I refer to as the action-belief dichotomy.

The right to religious freedom, which includes the right to hold religious beliefs and to practice in accordance with these beliefs, is also protected by:

> Article 18, International Covenant on Civil and Political Rights
>
> *1. Everyone shall have the right to freedom of thought, conscience and religion. The right shall include freedom to have or to adopt a religion or belief of his choice, and freedom, either individually or in community with others and in public or private, to manifest his religion or belief in worship, observance, practices and teaching.*
>
> *2. No one shall be subject to coercion which would impair his freedom to have or to adopt a religion or belief of his choice.*

Like the Declaration of Human Rights, paragraph 1 of Article 18 of the International Covenant on Civil and Political Rights (Covenant) specifically protects "religious belief" and "religious practice" or action, which is based on this belief. However, paragraph 3 of Article 18 of the Covenant also states that, *"Freedom to manifest* one's religion or beliefs may be subject only to such limitations as are prescribed by law and are necessary to protect public safety, order, health, or morals or the fundamental rights and freedoms of others." Paragraph 4 of Article 18 further declares that, "The States Parties to the present Covenant undertake to have respect for the liberty of parents and, when applicable, legal guardians to ensure the religious and moral education of their children in conformity with their own conviction."

The Covenant is a multilateral treaty adopted by the United Nations General Assembly on 16 December 1966. There is also the International Covenant on Economic, Social and Cultural Rights, Article 3 of which imposes an obligation on State parties to progressively realise the rights recognised in the Covenant "without discrimination of any kind as to ... religion".

3. The "action-belief" dichotomy

It is obvious that those who attack the Christian foundations of the common law rely on paragraph 3 of Article 18 of the Covenant to impose a secular agenda on Australia.

Critics of freedom of religion interpret the action-belief dichotomy as meaning that the legislator and the government's administrative apparatus are free to regulate, prohibit and even suppress religious practices which it deems to be inimical to State-determined priorities or social policy.

A classic description and example of the application of the action-belief dichotomy is found in the case of *Reynolds v United States*,[147] decided by the American Supreme Court in 1878. Reynolds, in obedience to the commands of his Mormon religion, which required Mormons to practice polygamy, had married a second

---

147 98 US 145 (1878).

wife. He justified his religious practice or action on the ground that it was the duty of a male Mormon to practice polygamy when circumstances permitted, and that refusal would be followed by damnation in the life to come. The Supreme Court, however, decided that, "Congress was deprived of all legislative power over mere opinion, but was left free to reach actions which were in violation of social duties or subversive of good order."

Although we might agree with the decision in *Reynolds*, reliance on paragraph 3 of Article 18 of the Covenant to suppress actions, which are deemed to subvert the social order, is problematic. This is because the usefulness of the action-belief dichotomy, which is embedded in paragraph 3, is constrained for several reasons, some of which I will now mention.

First, the position that a person's right to religious freedom does not restrict the competence of the State to regulate religious practice, was overhauled in 1972 in the iconic case of *Wisconsin v Yoder*.[148] In that case, the Supreme Court of the United States decided that religious practice is protected by the Constitution of the United States, at least in most circumstances, thereby effectively refining the action-belief dichotomy of *Reynolds v United States*.

Second, the action-belief dichotomy is conceptually unsound because the dichotomy cannot be used realistically in a pluralistic country like Australia that comprises many different religions. Indeed, the dichotomy can only be applied realistically in a religiously homogeneous society where it is possible to assess religiously inspired practices in the light of dominant community and religious values that exist in that homogeneous society. Thus, as most people disapproved of polygamy in the United States in the 19th century, it became easy as well as convenient for the Supreme

---

148   406 US 205 (1972).

Court to condemn the practice of polygamy.

Third, a major conceptual problem, inevitably associated with the application of the dichotomy, challenges our ability to make the dichotomy in the first place. Indeed, if a religious practice is regulated or prohibited, the belief upon which the action is based is, by implication, also deemed to be unreasonable. Thus, it may be argued that the dichotomy is artificial in the sense that empirically and logically, we cannot find that the belief upon which the practice is based, is unreasonable. Thus, I make the claim that religious practice cannot be separated from religious belief, and that if the practice is forbidden the belief itself is eroded. For example, Harrop A. Freeman argued in 1958 that every "great religion is not merely a matter of belief; it is action" and that one of the "most scathing rebukes in religion is reserved for hypocrites who believe but fail to so act".[149] Thus, religious belief and religious practice cannot neatly be separated from each other; rather they are stages of the one and indivisible reality: religious practice, or action, is articulated belief.

4. The Role of the West in the protection of religion

It is important to mention that the Western world has itself weakened its ability to protect the Christian foundations of the common law. This is because the West has progressively devalued the importance and the role of religion in Western society. The fact that religion in our secular society is being devalued, must necessarily impact on our ability, or even willingness, to condemn persecution of religion and people of faith. Subject to the validity of this point, the West may find it difficult, for example, to criticise

---

149 Harrop A Freeman, "A Remonstrance for Conscience", 106 *University of Pennsylvania Law Review* 806, 1958, 826.

and condemn the persecution of religious minorities in Iran and Yemen where religious minorities, such as the members of the Baha'i faith, are treated abominably and imprisoned.

In 2004 I published an article entitled *The Menace of Neutrality in Religion* in the Brigham Young University Law Review.[150] The article deals essentially with the conflict between religion, on the one hand, and the demands and expectations of our secular world, on the other. Specifically, it concerns the role that religion and religious discourse play in the public forum. In the article I noted that church attendance has substantially collapsed in most Western countries. In addition, many leaders of established religions are no longer able, or willing, to serve as moral standard bearers.[151] Indeed, even a perfunctory review of the state of religion in Western societies reveals that organised religions are in turmoil which, at least in part, is a consequence of the seeming inability of religious leaders to support the moral foundations and tenets of their own faith. Now, 16 years later, the situation described in 2004 has only worsened as is evidenced by the public investigations into child sexual abuse committed by priests and the revelations made in the Royal Commission into Institutional Responses to Child Sexual Abuse in Australia (and similar enquiries in a number of other countries as well). There is no doubt that organised religions, or "churches". have lost their erstwhile authority and moral supremacy in an increasingly secular world. My point is that the collapse of religion and religious practice in Australia and other Western countries has, in effect, adversely affected our ability to halt the erosion of the Christian foundations of the common law, and the discrimination of religious groups around the world. The secularisation process has made us largely indifferent to our own

---

[150] Gabriël A. Moens, "The Menace of Neutrality in Religion", 2004(2), *Brigham Young University Law Review*, 2004, 535-574.

[151] *Ibid.*, 535.

heritage and the plight of religious minorities.

What should be the appropriate response to the obvious decline of religion and the associated crisis of faith in the Western world? I my opinion, the response should not be to abandon religion, but to maintain the faith upon which one's religion is based. This is because most of the criticism directed at religion confounds "church" and "religion" and erroneously uses these two nouns interchangeably. A church and their church leaders could behave demonically, but this does not prove that religion is bad for society. Indeed, the obnoxious behaviour of some church leaders should not be used as a reason for abandoning religion and for denigrating the valuable role that religion continues to make to the maintenance of a decent and civilised society under the rule of law. Indeed, it is perfectly possible to condemn the detestable attitudes and repugnant behaviour of errant church leaders and individual members of a religion, whilst at the same time champion and nurture the role that religious faith plays in society and in individuals' lives.

Whereas an organised religion, or "church", is predominantly a collection of people who profess the same faith, religion is an intensively personal activity even if it is exercised in community with others. Religion involves the relationship between individuals and a Supreme Being. Hence, it is entirely possible for a person to be anti-church, but still be religious and spiritual, thereby maintaining their ability to deplore the loss of our knowledge of the Christian foundations of the common law and the persecution of people of faith.

There are many other international documents which protect the right to religious freedom, including the rights to hold religious beliefs and the right to practice these beliefs. For example, the Declaration on the Elimination of All Forms of Intolerance and of

Discrimination Based on Religion and Belief was adopted by the General Assembly of the United Nations on 25 November 1981. Article 3 of this Declaration stipulates that, "Discrimination between human beings on the ground of religion or belief constitutes an affront to human dignity and a disavowal of the principles of the Charter of the United Nations, and shall be condemned as a violation of the human rights and fundamental freedoms proclaimed in the Universal Declaration of Human Rights and enunciated in detail in the International Covenants on Human Rights and as an obstacle to friendly and peaceful relations between nations." In addition, there are many regional documents that protect religious belief and practice. They include Article 10, Charter of Fundamental Rights of the European Union, and Article 9, European Convention on Human Rights. Although these documents are not directly relevant to our Australian context, it is useful to mention that they expressly protect the right to religious belief and practice.

My message, I hope is clear: discrimination on grounds of religion is, using the language of the 1981 Declaration, "an affront to human dignity." It is incompatible with international human rights standards which protect religious belief and religious practice. Religion should be revalued in the Western world, including in Australia, to ensure that this message can be made strongly, confidently, and loudly.

This, then, is the important and lasting contribution made by *The Christian Foundations of the Common Law*: this excellent book is a timely reminder of the Christian heritage of the common law that has served us so well for more than two centuries. It is erudite, informative, well-written and researched. Indeed, it might serve as the ideal literature for the Christmas season that is not too far off.

14

THE PROTECTION OF PUBLIC HEALTH:
REFLECTIONS ON THE COVID-19 VIRUS PANDEMIC AND THE ROLE OF THE STATE

(2020)

1. Covid-19 as a Disrupter of Life

The Covid-19 virus, popularly known as the coronavirus, apparently entered Australia sometime in January 2020, possibly by plane coming from Wuhan, Hubei Province, People's Republic of China. It was in Wuhan that the ravages caused by this virus were first experienced among the local population. Since then, the virus spread to most countries and resulted in approximately 4 million of infections; close to 350,000 deaths were attributed to the disease. The World Health Organization (WHO) declared a Public Health Emergency of International Concern on 30 January 2020.

The Commonwealth Government of Australia responded to this unprecedented virus threat to the health of people by instituting a National Cabinet, consisting of the Prime Minister and the Premiers of the States and the Chief Ministers of Territories, assisted by the Chief Medical Officer, to design a joint and co-ordinated response to the spread of the virus. Specifically, to slow down the transmission of the disease by humans to other humans, the Australian Federal, State and Territory governments adopted some of the most restrictive laws on movement. By any standard, the measures taken were draconian: States and Territories effectively closed their borders, meetings of more than ten people were banned in some States and people over 70 were encouraged, if not ordered, to stay at home. Food and medicines were delivered to people's houses and physical contact, even with children and grandchildren, was discouraged. People were expected to practice "social distancing" which means that people must maintain a distance of at least 1,5 metres from other people.

Importantly, in closing down businesses, cancelling events, stopping international travel and most of domestic travel, this Cabinet created an unemployment crisis of immense proportions; more than one million people lost their jobs, at least temporarily, making it difficult for many to pay their rents or mortgages. All the resources of government are commandeered to fight the disease. The Government undertook to spend a staggering amount of money, more than $200 billion, to protect the sovereignty of Australia and to ensure that business can return to normal once the crisis passes. This treasure chest is used to provide temporary monetary support to workers who became unemployed when businesses closed; this is known as the JobKeeper scheme. Childcare centres are subsidised to ensure they stay open; private hospitals are brought under public control, and many people now work from home.

Australian governments started to relax some of these restrictions in early May 2020, but it is expected that a return to normal will only be gradual and some restrictions will be in place for a long time, for example, the ban on international travel. The ubiquitous handshake, which probably originated in the 5th century B.C. in Greece, has become a notorious casualty of the virus, being replaced by a bumping of the elbows.

This unprecedented situation prods me into considering the role of the State in this crisis. I have always been interested, intellectually and practically, in the proper role of the State in society, but I have pursued this interest in the context of a coronavirus-free environment. Specifically, in 2014 I published a paper that deals with the role of the State in the protection of peoples' health in which I argue that governments, rather than prescriptively prohibiting unwanted behaviour ("Nanny State" measures), have recourse to more subtle, but equally effective, forms of social control ("Nudge State" measures) that purport to maintain personal choice.[152] However, the Covid-19 pandemic has completely changed this narrative on the issues discussed in that paper and, hence, it is appropriate, useful as well as topical to include a substantially revised version of this paper in this Collection.

In this paper, I trace the journey of State interventionism involving the legislative adoption of behavioural rules to improve public health. In the pre-Covid-19 era, "Nudge State" interventionism was the preferred legislative approach to controlling the health of citizens. However, since the outbreak of the Covid-19 pandemic and the staggering rivers of cash thrown at its defeat, it is clear that the "Nanny State" approach is prevalent and that any Nudge State measures are merely convenient smokescreens used in less challenging times to control the health of a State's population.

In this paper, I propose to examine how the "Nudge State" approach differs, if at all, from the "Nanny State" approach, and how

---

[152] Gabriël A. Moens and Rajesh Sharma, "Improving Public Health Through Behavioural Rules: A Legitimate Legislative Project of a Nanny State or a Nudge State?" 57 (4) *Journal of the Indian Law Institute*, 2015, 474-498.

the Covid-19 virus pandemic has made this debate largely academic. Specifically, I will argue that the distinction between the Nanny State and Nudge State is a distinction without a difference and that the Covid-19 pandemic has resulted in the restoration of an extreme version of the "Nanny State" approach.

2. The "Nanny State" and the "Nudge" State: A Distinction without a Difference?

Since the Second World War, governments have intervened legislatively and administratively to ensure that citizens are properly protected against health risks. This intervention led to the creation of the "Nanny State'" which essentially replaced the free choice of individuals with the decision-making power of the government. In pre-Covid-19 days, this intervention generated a discussion about the extent to which governments should embrace paternalism as a principle of legislation. The implementation of this principle resulted in the imposition of unpopular and burdensome health regulations because it validated the making of decisions which individuals should be allowed to make themselves. For this reason, supporters of "Nanny State" interventionism sought to moderate their approach through the medium of a "Nudge State", though in goal and philosophy they are similar. This similarity arises from the fact that the Nudge State seeks to achieve the same objectives, not by prescriptively controlling, forbidding or compelling the behaviour of individuals (as is usual under Nanny State interventionism), but by making this behaviour economically expensive, socially undesirable or emotionally challenging.

The term "Nanny State" is a familiar description of the tendency of many modern governments to treat their "citizens as children in a nursery",[153] supervising and influencing their choices according to the government's view of their well-being. Such an approach is "authoritarian and paternalistic ... imposing on people what is good for them, for 'nanny knows best'."[154]

In contrast, the supporters of the "Nudge State" approach seek to make Nanny less prominent by seeking to preserve free choice. They rather wordily define a "nudge" as "any aspect of the choice architecture that alters people's behavior in a predictable way without forbidding any options or significantly changing their economic incentives".[155] According to Richard Thaler, the Nanny State is coercive, for example by banning cigarettes, while the Nudge State seeks to goad people in a pre-determined direction that is favoured by the State, for example, by quitting smoking.[156] The Nudge State philosophy thus seeks to manipulate and influence peoples' choices, not by banning these choices, but by making it more difficult to freely choose or by making the choice economically prohibitive, socially undesirable, or emotionally challenging. As such, although Nanny does not make the decisions, for example, that people should not smoke, it nevertheless influences and manipulates individuals' choices to smoke.

The Nudge State approach is zealously paternalistic: "At the core of nudging is the belief that people do not always act in their own self-interest."[157] Underlying that philosophy is the notion that the State

---

153 R W Holder, *How Not To Say What You Mean: A Dictionary of Euphemisms* (4th ed), Oxford: Oxford University Press, 2007, 269.
154 John Ayto and Ian Crofton, *Brewer's Dictionary of Modern Phrase and Fable* (2nd ed), London: Weidenfeld & Nicolson, 2006, 520.
155 Richard H Thaler and Cass R Sunstein, *Nudge: Improving Decisions about Health, Wealth, and Happiness*, New Haven, Conn: Yale University Press, 2008, 5-6.
156 Interview with Richard Thaler, *HARDtalk*, BBC World Service, 24 October 2012, available at http://www.bbc.co.uk/podcasts/series/ht/all.
157 Katrin Bennhold, "The Ministry of Nudges", *New York Times*, 8 December 2013, BU1.

can make better choices for citizens than those citizens will make for themselves if left to their own devices. This worldview seeks to protect consumers even where they do not want protection, "overriding consumer preferences to improve public health."[158]

A patronising sense of entitlement to a guiding role over the lives of others pervades the policies of a Nudge State. The Nudge State seeks to "coax and cajole ... autonomous adults into healthier decision making"[159] and "to steer citizens towards making positive decisions as individuals and for society."[160] Although the changes to the choice architecture of society might appear to be minimal, their cumulative effect is to significantly shift the behaviour of people in the direction favoured by governments.[161]

The Nudge approach even made its presence felt in the formal structure of government. The British coalition government, led by former Prime Minister David Cameron, established a Behavioural Insights Team, popularly known as the "Nudge Unit". This unit attempts to apply insights from behavioural psychology to the development of policy, seeking to influence individual behaviour to ensure its compatibility with government policy objectives. The State thus employs people who are actively charged with dreaming up new ways to interfere in the lives of ordinary people. The Unit's Internet blog ranges over the staggeringly wide field in which they offer their valuable insights: from obesity, tax compliance, literacy, numeracy, organ donation, household appliances, loft insulation,

---

[158] Katherine Pratt, "A Constructive Critique of Public Health Arguments for Antiobesity Soda Taxes and Food Taxes" 87 *Tulane Law Review*, 2012, 73, 107.
[159] Jonathan Cummings, "Obesity and Unhealthy Consumption: The Public-Policy Case for Placing a Federal Sin Tax on Sugary Beverages" 34 *Seattle University Law Review*, 2010, 273, 294.
[160] Alberto Alemanno, "Nudging Smokers: The Behavioural Turn of Tobacco Risk Regulation" *European Journal of Risk Regulation*, 2012-1, 32, 32.
[161] Helen Lewis, "Out of the Ordinary", *New Statesman*, 30 September-6 October 2016, 23.

mobile phone theft, Christmas presents, plastic shopping bags, staircases, and penalty shoot-outs.[162] In the United States, President Barrack Obama issued an Executive Order mandating the use of behavioural science in policymaking.[163]

But in general, there is little difference in substance between the "Nanny State" and the "Nudge State". The Nudge State is simply an attempt to rebrand the way in which governments seek to influence the choices made by their citizens. As the Nanny State has been rejected by the citizenry because of its paternalistic characteristics, a Nudge State government seeks to promote its preferred choices by manipulating the choice. In doing so, Nudge State governments often adversely impact on the rights and interests of the suppliers of these choices. Thus, the Nanny State and the Nudge State legislative programmes are both based on, and inspired by, the same "nanny knows best" philosophy. Essentially, it is a distinction without a difference.

For example, government policymakers may assume, perhaps correctly, that people in general are addicted to soft drinks which contain a high level of sugar, which contributes to obesity. This, in turn, may facilitate the introduction of Nudge State measures, including the imposition of production specifications, that result in substantially increasing the price of these products. In this sense, a Nudge measure is a short cut which enables governments to achieve policy objectives, and targets, in an expedient manner, perceived social ills without having to rely on the cumulative effect of private choices which are made by people.

---

162 http://www.behaviouralinsights.co.uk/blog.
163 Executive Order 13707, "Using Behavioral Science Insights to Better Serve the American People.", 15 September 2015. The Order requires federal agencies to integrate behavioural insights into their policies and programmes; it also establishes the Social and Behavioral Sciences Team (SBST).

In contrast, a libertarian philosophy and approach provide an alternative to the implementation of the principle of paternalism. According to libertarian philosophy, it is not the role of the State to hold the hands of adults of full capacity as they make their way through commercial life. This libertarian philosophy emphasises both personal choice and acceptance of individual responsibility for the consequences of those choices: "people should be free to choose whether to live in ways that are healthy or unhealthy and take personal responsibility for their own health."[164]

Every time the government seeks to mould individual economic and social choices, personal freedom is diminished, hence strong justifications should be proffered for such interventions. Intervention should be a last resort, not a reflex instinct. Most "Nanny State" or "Nudge State" interventions take place by way of legislation, rather than judge-made law. Many rules of the common law and equity have libertarian characteristics, generally holding parties to their bargains and resisting the temptation to abolish or revise obligations freely undertaken merely because their outcomes subsequently prove disadvantageous to a party. In contrast, the legislative and executive branches of many governments in Western countries appear to be faithfully devoted to Nudge State interventions.

One of the most controversial "Nudge State" interventions is the Australian federal law which provides that tobacco products may be sold only in generic packaging. The exterior of Australian cigarette packs must be "dark drab brown" in colour and have a matt finish.[165] The executively mandated specific colour is re-

---

164 Pratt, *supra* n. 158, 110, 129.
165 s 19(1)-(2), *Tobacco Plain Packaging Act* 2011 (Cth).

puted to be the "world's ugliest colour".[166] The interior of packs must be white.[167] The legislation effectively guts valuable tobacco trademarks of any economic significance. Trademarks may not appear on cigarette packaging, other than a single use of the brand name.[168] Even the size, typeface and colour of the brand name are closely regulated.[169] Trademarks may not appear on the cigarettes themselves[170] or the packet wrappers.[171] Ugly graphic health warnings must take up 75% of the front of packets and 90 % of their reverse side.[172]

3. Policy Considerations: The Futility of "Nanny State" and "Nudge State" Measures

There are numerous policy objections to most paternalistic "Nanny State" and "Nudge State" interventions, for example, the ready alternative of promoting and accepting individual responsibility, the substitution effect, the probable circumvention of such laws, the likelihood of unintended consequences, the availability of voluntary alternatives, the lack of public support for

---

166 Rachel Wells, "Does this colour turn you off?", *The Age*, 17 August 2012. The specific colour is set by the regulations (Pantone 448C). See r 2.2.1(2), *Tobacco Plain Packaging Regulations* 2011 (Cth).
167 r 2.2.1(3), *Tobacco Plain Packaging Regulations* 2011 (Cth).
168 ss 20(1), (3), 21(2)(b), *Tobacco Plain Packaging Act* 2011 (Cth).
169 r 2.4.1, *Tobacco Plain Packaging Regulations* 2011 (Cth).
170 s 26(1), *Tobacco Plain Packaging Act* 2011 (Cth).
171 s 22(2)(b), *Tobacco Plain Packaging Act* 2011 (Cth).
172 ss 9.13(1), 9.19(1), *Competition and Consumer (Tobacco) Information Standard* 2011 (Cth) (Federal Register of Legislative Instruments F2013C00598). In 2015, the Australian Capital Territory government decided to ban advertisements for fossil fuels, junk food, alcohol, gambling, or defence industries on Canberra's public buses. The government argued that this "Nanny State" measure ensures that the products which are promoted on buses are appropriate for the broader populations and are in line with the values of the Canberra community and government objectives.

such measures and the likelihood of endless litigation challenging Nanny State and Nudge State impositions. As it is conceptually difficult to distinguish "Nudge State" and "Nanny State" measures, these objections may equally apply to both types of impositions.

It is often argued that Nanny State and Nudge State measures against obesity are warranted because obesity results in higher health costs which are absorbed by private or public health insurance companies. However, these costs could arguably be minimised if the health insurance industry were to price insurance premiums in line with individual risk, so that those who are obese would pay higher premiums since their treatment costs are likely to be more expensive than those of non-obese persons.[173]

Such measures would certainly be controversial and sensitive because those who pay the higher premiums would claim to be the victim of unjustifiable discrimination. Nevertheless, this approach would send a strong price signal against obesity and is consistent with individual responsibility for health because a large proportion of obesity cases are the result of individual lifestyle choices. The prospect of paying a financial penalty would function as a constant economic disincentive against an unhealthy lifestyle. Such an approach is supported by research suggesting that most people are more likely to modify their behaviour in response to a financial loss than to achieve an economic gain.[174]

When a tax is imposed upon a good, people tend to substitute an alternative that has similar qualities or effects. For example, raising the price of alcohol has often been followed by an increase in the consumption of marijuana as one drug is substituted for

---

[173] Alexander Copp, "The Ethics and Efficacy of a 'Fat Tax' in the Form of an Insurance Surcharge on Obese State Employees", 15(1) *Quinnipiac Health Law Journal*, 2012, 8-10.

[174] Copp, *supra* n. 173, 25.

the other.[175] This effect has also been observed in the case of food. While soda taxes reduce the consumption of soda, consumers substitute other high calorie drinks, with the result that there is no reduction in the obesity rate.[176] This is exactly what economic theory predicts will occur in these cases.[177] Furthermore, alcohol taxes drastically reduce consumption by light drinkers but have little effect upon consumption by heavy drinkers.[178]

Sometimes, consumers do not even need to substitute a different food. It is also often easy for consumers to circumvent a tax. For example, a Danish fat tax was circumvented by Danish consumers buying high fat foods in neighbouring Germany and Sweden where the prices were lower.[179] The American "no free toys" ordinances, which prohibited fast food restaurants from serving food and offering free toys to children, were quickly circumvented by charging a nominal fee for the toys, thereby bypassing the nutritional strictures.

Many Nanny State and Nudge State measures have unintended consequences. Stricter anti-obesity laws have been associated with an increase in the social stigma attached to obesity. Furthermore, obesity rates did not actually decline.[180] Punitive measures against obese people may also be challenged as infringements of anti-

---

175 Alemanno, *supra* n 160, 100.
176 Jonathan Klick and Erich A Helland, "Slim Odds", 34 *Regulation* 20, Spring 2011; Susan Yeh, "Laws and Social Norms: Unintended Consequences of Obesity Laws", 81 *University of Cincinnati Law Review*, 2012, 173, 184.
177 Michael L Marlow and Alden F Shiers, "Would Soda Taxes Really Yield Health Benefits?", 33 *Regulation* 34, Fall 2010, 37.
178 Marlow and Shiers, *supra* n. 177, 37.
179 Stephanie Strom, "Fat Foods Tax is Repealed in Denmark", *New York Times*, 13 November 2012, B4; Sarah Kliff, "Denmark scraps world's first fat tax", *Washington Post*, 13 November 2012.
180 Yeh, *supra* n. 176, 176, 211; Alberto Alemanno and Amandine Garde, "The Emergence of an EU Lifestyle Policy: The Case of Alcohol, Tobacco and Unhealthy Diets", 50 *Common Market Law Review*, 2013, 1745, 1759.

discrimination laws.[181] To provide another example, soda taxes target beverages generally favoured by the poor rather than those favoured by the rich, though the calorie content of each drink may be similar.[182]

Such State measures do not arise from popular demand. Where voters have been given a direct choice about Nanny State and Nudge State measures, they have usually rejected such interventions. For example, in several American States, soda taxes have been repealed at state-wide referenda.[183] That is not surprising in view of the fact that, usually, individuals do not want the government instructing them what to eat and charging them more if they chose something that is deemed to be unhealthy.

If business is subject to onerous regulation, it will naturally seek to challenge those rules. Extensive litigation is thus the inevitable result of the adoption of Nudge State and Nanny State policies. An instructive example of this is offered by the tobacco industry which has been subject to numerous restrictive Nudge State and Nanny State interventions. The industry's response was litigation seeking to defend its interests. Indeed, the scale of litigation regarding tobacco restrictions has been extensive. Nations with tobacco industries and the industry itself have challenged restrictive legislation under international trade law, European Union law, international investment protection law, European

---

181 Nola M Ries, "Legal and Policy Measures to Promote Healthy Behaviour: Using Incentives and Disincentives to Control Obesity, 6 *McGill Journal of Law and Health*, 2012, 1, 34-36.
182 Chris L Winstanley, "A Healthy Food Tax Credit: Moving Away from the Fat Tax and Its Fault-Based Paradigm", 86 *Oregon Law Review*, 2007, 1151, 175-1176; Trevor Burrus, "The Dangers of a Soda Tax", 29 November 2013, http://www.cato.org/blog/dangers-soda-tax.
183 J Angelo DeSantis, "Formulating A Soda Tax Fit For Consumption: A Pragmatic Approach to Implementing the Failed New York Soda Tax", 16 *Michigan State University Journal of Medicine and Law*, 2012, 363, 398-399.

Free Trade Association law, European human rights law, and national constitutional law.

The first investor-state dispute, brought against Australia in the Permanent Court of Arbitration was the Philip Morris Asia case which was arbitrated under the *Agreement between the Government of Australia and the Government of Hong Kong for the Promotion and Protection of Investments* which entered into force on 15 October 1993. It followed a decision by the Australian High Court on the constitutionality of the *Tobacco Plain Packaging Act 2011* (Cth).[184] The High Court had decided that s 51(xxxi) of the Commonwealth Constitution had not been violated because the interest or benefit obtained by the Commonwealth was not proprietary in nature.[185] The Arbitral Tribunal decided on 18 December 2015 that it did not have jurisdiction to hear Philip Morris Asia's claim. In reasons, published on 17 May 2016, it found that the claim constituted an abuse of process, specifically an abuse of rights, because Philip Morris Asia had acquired an Australian subsidiary, Philip Morris (Australia), for the specific purpose of enabling it to initiate arbitration under the Hong Kong Agreement to challenge Australia's tobacco laws.[186] The response of the former Australian Gillard Labor government was simply to announce that it would no longer accept investor-state arbitration mechanisms in future

---

[184] *JT International SA v Commonwealth*, 250 CLR 1 (2012). See generally, Meika Atkins, "Australia's Restrictive Tobacco Laws: Are Australia's Trade Agreements Going Up in Smoke", XXI *International Trade and Business Law Review* 333, 2018.

[185] See for a discussion of this case, Gabriël A Moens and John Trone, *The Constitution of the Commonwealth of Australia Annotated*, 9th ed, LexisNexis Butterworths, 2016, 197-198.

[186] *Philip Morris Asia Ltd (Hong Kong) v Australia* (PCA Case 2012-12). See for a discussion of this case, Vivienne Bath and Gabriël Moens, *Law of International Business in Australasia*, 2nd ed, The Federation Press, 2019, 520-521.

treaties.[187]

The Australian plain packaging legislation was the subject of five disputes under the World Trade Organization dispute settlement framework.[188] These cases were decided in favour of Australia in 2018. In June 2014, Philip Morris International also brought an action in a British court seeking a preliminary ruling concerning the validity of the new European Union Tobacco Products Directive.[189]

4. The Covid-19 Challenge

It was argued in the previous section that "Nudge State" interventionism in the field of public health is the functional equivalent of "Nanny State" interventionism. These measures, regardless of the form they take, have effectively removed from individuals the power to make their own health decisions. Although several objections to paternalistic Nudge State and Nanny State interventions were discussed and assessed above, the State determinedly pursues these policies, presumably to maintain the health of its citizens. A

---

[187] Jürgen Kurtz, "Australia's Rejection of Investor–State Arbitration: Causation, Omission and Implication", 27 *ICSID Review*, 2012, 65. In contrast, the Coalition federal government has indicated that it would consider the inclusion of such clauses on a case by case basis. See Leon E Trakman, "Investor-State Arbitration: Evaluating Australia's Evolving Position", 15 *Journal of World Investment and Trade*, 2014, 152; Luke Nottage, "The 'Anti-ISDS Bill' Before the Senate: What Future for Investor-State Arbitration in Australia?", XVIII *International Trade and Business Law Review*, 2015, 245-293.

[188] DS434 (Ukraine), DS435 (Honduras), DS441 (Dominican Republic), DS458 (Cuba), DS467 (Indonesia). However, an appeal to the Appellate Body by Honduras and the Dominican Republic have not yet been released. See summary on DFAT website at https://dfat.gov.au. A discussion on the WTO's dispute settlement process may be found in Vivienne Bath and Gabriël Moens, supra n. 186, 514-521.

[189] Directive 2014/40 of the European Parliament and of the Council of 3 April 2014 on the approximation of the laws, regulations and administrative provisions of the Member States concerning the manufacture, presentation and sale of tobacco and related products, OJ L 127, 29.4.2014, 1.

staggering amount of legislation relating to the Covid-19 pandemic has already been adopted.[190]

The current Covid-19 pandemic, however, has exposed the irrelevance of any attempts to ascertain sophisticated differences between Nudge State and Nanny State measures. The Federal Government, in adopting draconian legislation to combat the virus, has once again resorted to conventional, prescriptive Nanny State measures which, however, have the potential to seriously impact on the enjoyment of civil liberties, and generally, respect for the rule of law. This is because these measures have substantially increased the discretionary power of the police, who may well assume that people are presumed guilty of violating social distancing rules, non-essential travel restrictions, and isolation requirements, all of which might result in the imposition of hefty fines.[191]

These unprecedented restrictions on the enjoyment of our civil liberties has been criticised, notably by Professor Augusto Zimmermann in *Quadrant Online*, on the ground that it involves decision making by Diktat. In his comment, *Government by Virus and Executive Diktat*[192] of 8 April 2020, he deplores the diminished authority of the Parliament and the erosion of the separation of powers doctrine, and he describes the actions of governments as more suitable to totalitarian regimes:

---

190 Biosecurity Act 2015 (Cth) (Compilation as at 1 March 2019); Biosecurity (Human Biosecurity Emergency) (Human Coronavirus with Pandemic Potential) (Emergency Requirements for Remote Communities) Amendment (No. 1) Determination 2020, 7 April 2020; Biosecurity (Exit Requirements) Amendment (Nauru) Determination 2020, 2 April 2020.

191 It is ironic that these measures taken to protect the health of citizens may have the unintended effect of diluting the quality of medical services in Australia. Indeed, the Government-approved medical service delivery by telephone has made it more difficult to secure a face-to-face appointment with a medical practitioner in a timely manner.

192 *Quadrant Online*, 8 April 2020.

Because these extreme measures are dictated by the executive and have no deadline to expire, we are effectively experiencing government by executive decree. This is something akin to the actions of deeply authoritarian regimes, in particular when such executive measures are not properly scrutinised.

Professor Zimmermann, whilst admitting that sometimes emergency powers are needed, maintains that the current measures "will dramatically increase the power of the state, thus allowing governments to arbitrarily exercise mass surveillance powers" resulting in alarming restriction of civil liberties and that, "any rush to embrace draconian measures in our response to the present crisis will give the state terrifyingly broad powers." In using these powers, governments have adopted measures which have devastated the entire economy. Potentially, the collapse of the economy has terrifying concomitant consequences:

> Inevitably, job losses will lead to far more homelessness, with financial pressures leading to a much higher suicide rate, widespread marriage breakdown and to a dramatic growth in crime, which always increases in times of economic crisis.[193]

He argues for a proportionate response to the crisis. His assessment is clear:

> Yes, coronavirus poses a serious public health risk. But the key word here is proportion. These draconian measures provide a pretext for the authoritarian takeover of civil society that not only unleashes unprecedented economic mayhem, but also threatens our present way of life and what it means to live in a free and democratic society.[194]

In Australia, the legislative power to combat Covid-19 belongs to

---

193 *Quadrant Online*, 5 April 2020.
194 *Quadrant Online*, 5 April 2020.

the States and Territories.¹⁹⁵ Hence, each jurisdiction has adopted relevant emergency legislation.¹⁹⁶ However, it might be argued that the "nationhood" power which is based on s 61 of the Commonwealth Constitution according to which "The executive power of the Commonwealth ... extends to the execution and maintenance of this Constitution, and of the laws of the Commonwealth." provides a justification for the introduction of Commonwealth-sponsored emergency measures.

It is likely that the emergency measures introduced by the Commonwealth are constitutional as suggested in *Pape v Federal Commissioner of Taxation*, decided by the High Court in 2009.¹⁹⁷ *Pape* dealt with the Global Financial Crisis and the economic stimulus law adopted by the Parliament. In *Pape*, the Commonwealth argued that such law was supported by an implied legislative "nationhood power". Although a majority of the High Court (French CJ, Gummow, Crennan and Bell JJ) found it unnecessary to consider this issue,¹⁹⁸ it was held that the *Tax Bonus for Working Australians Act (No 2) 2009* (Cth), which authorised the appropriation of money from consolidated revenue to make stimulus payments to individual taxpayers was constitutionally valid under s. 51(xxxix) of the Constitution, namely the incidental power to the exercise of the executive power. Gummow, Crennan and Bell JJ stated that, "The Executive Government is the arm of government capable of and empowered to respond to a crisis be it war, natural disaster or a

---

195 Australian Institute for Disaster Resilience, "Australian Emergency Management Arrangements, Department of Home Affairs, 2019, 4.
196 See *Emergencies Act 2004 (ACT)*; *State Emergency and Rescue Management Act 1989* (NSW); *Emergency Management Act 2013* (NT); *Disaster Management Act 2003* (Qld); *Emergency Management Act 2004* (SA); *Emergency Management Act 2006* (Tas); *Emergency Management Act 1986* (Vic); *Emergency Management Act 2013* (Vic); *Emergency Management Act 2005* (WA).
197 238 CLR 1 (2009). See on this case, Gabriël A Moens and John Trone, *supra* n. 185, 2016, 233.
198 *Supra* n. 197, 133.

financial crisis on the scale here."[199] Importantly, French CJ reassuringly indicated that, "the exigencies of 'national government' cannot be invoked to set aside the distribution of powers between Commonwealth and States and between the three branches of government for which this Constitution provides, nor to abrogate constitutional prohibitions."

In his dissent, Heydon J pointed out that the mere fact that a matter is one of national interest does not mean that it necessarily falls within an implied nationhood power.[200] He opposed a substantial extension of Commonwealth powers in this interesting passage from his judgment:

> The truth is that the modern world is in part created by the way language is used. Modern linguistic usage suggests that the present age is one of "emergencies", "crises", "dangers" and "intense difficulties", of "scourges" and other problems. They relate to things as diverse as terrorism, water shortages, drug abuse, child abuse, poverty, pandemics, obesity, and global warming, as well as global financial affairs. In relation to them, the public is endlessly told, "wars" must be waged, "campaigns" conducted, "strategies" devised and "battles" fought. Often these problems are said to arise suddenly and unexpectedly. Sections of the public constantly demand urgent action to meet particular problems. The public is continually told that it is facing "decisive" junctures, "crucial" turning points and "critical" decisions. Even if only a narrow power to deal with an emergency on the scale of the global financial crisis were recognised, it would not take long before constitutional lawyers and politicians between them managed to convert that power into something capable of almost daily use. The great maxim of governments seeking to widen their constitutional powers would be: "Never allow a

---

199 *Supra* n. 197, 89 (Gummow, Crennan and Bell JJ).
200 *Supra* n. 197, 504.

crisis to go to waste.'

Justice Heydon's sentiment is reinforced in a powerful comment, published in *Quadrant Online* by Professor Zimmermann:

> ... many Australians have developed an utterly distorted view of what governments can do for them. Such individuals now blindly worship at the altar of the all-powerful State, expecting it to be their almighty saviour, seeing in government the ultimate provider for all things. Perhaps this is a result of society's lost faith in the God of Christianity. Be that as it may, the undeniable truth is that far too many Australians have acquired an unshakable faith in their political class. Call it a form of idolatry if you wish.[201]

It will be interesting to see how the Covid-19 crisis unfolds and what the lasting consequences will be for the protection of citizens' civil rights and the rule of law in Australia. Justice Heydon's admonition that governments could convert emergency powers into "something capable of almost daily use", and Professor Zimmermann's assessment that citizens have acquired an unrealistic view of what governments can do for them are important reminders of the innate dangers associated with this pandemic. But for now, it is undeniable that Nanny has triumphed![202]

---

201 Augusto Zimmermann, "In the State you will Trust", *Quadrant Online*, 15 April 2020.

202 As this Chapter was submitted to the publisher in the middle of May 2020, it does not offer an account of the many developments which occurred after that date. Since then, there has been a serious outbreak of the virus in Victoria that adopted harsh lock-down measures, and in Sydney. The number of infections has also sharply risen in overseas countries. An account of the pandemic until the middle of August 2020 is offered in a book edited by Professor Augusto Zimmermann, and entitled Fundamental Rights in the Age of Covid-19, Connor Court Publishing, 2020. This book also contains a Review of Moens' debut novel, A Twisted Choice - A Covid-19 Novel.

15

NEDERLANDS: DE TAAL VAN DE GEMISTE KANSEN (DUTCH: THE LANGUAGE OF MISSED OPPORTUNITIES)

(1980)

1. Nederlands: een potentiële wereldtaal

Indien het Nederlands zich had kunnen handhaven waar het werd gesproken en gebruikt, dan zou het nu ongetwijfeld een wereldtaal geweest zijn. Door het feit dat dit niet gebeurd is kunnen wij het Nederlands zien als de taal van de gemiste kansen. In mijn lezing vandaag zal ik zoeken naar de redenen waarom de Nederlandse taal en kultuur zich niet heeft kunnen handhaven.

De Nederlandse taal en kultuur heeft nochtans in vele delen van de wereld bruggehoofden gehad. De groeikiemen nodig voor het uitbouwen van een wereldtaal waren sinds de late middeleeuwen wel aanwezig. Zo heeft het Nederlands een belangrijke en merkwaardige invloed gehad op verscheidene andere talen. Peter de Grote van Rusland was een bewonderaar van de Nederlandse scheepsvaart. Het Nederlands werd ook toonaangevend in de Russische scheepsvaartterminologie. Er zijn nog minstens 156 zeemanstermen van Nederlandse oorsprong in de Russische taal, zoals "matroos" en "vaarwater". Verder zijn russische woorden op het gebied van koophandel en nijverheid aan het Nederlands ontleend. In totaal zijn er nog een zes- to zevenhonderd gangbare Russische woorden van Nederlandse oorsprong.

Verder heeft het Nederlands een merkwaardige bekendheid genoten in de Scandinavische landen. Vooral de Nederlandse invloed op het Deens is zeer duidelijk in de 16de, 17de en 18de eeuw. Het Nederlands was er veel invloedrijker dan de grote cultuurtalen. Lange tijd werden Nederlandse toneelstukken in Kopenhagen opgevoerd en meer dan duizend zee- en scheepsvaarttermen zijn aan het Nederlands ontleend. In Nederlands-Indië was het Nederlands gedurende drie eeuwen de taal van de administratie en de protestantse kerk, maar door de blanken werden geen pogingen ondernomen om de bevolking te vernederlandsen.

In de Nederlandse Antillen is het Nederlands de officiële taal gebleven nadat interne zelfstandigheid werd verworven. Het Nederlands is er de regeringtaal en protestantse kerktaal, maar het heeft nooit wortel geschoten bij de bevolking die Papiamentoe spreekt.

Ook Ceylon (Sri Lanka) was van 1656 to 1803 een Nederlandse kolonie, maar nadat dit gebied in de handen kwam van Engeland heeft het Nederlands er zich niet gehandhaaft. Er zijn wel nog sporen van het Nederlands terugtevinden in de inheemse taal, het Singhalees, zoals kalabere (klaveren), kerrekoppe (Kerkhof) en tarappe (trap).

Ik zou ook kunnen spreken over de Azoren, die in de vijftiende eeuw door Zuid-Nederlanders werden gekoloniseerd; over het feit dat Cromwell en Milton Nederlands konden spreken; over de kolonisatie van, en emigratie naar, Noord-Amerika en hoe Nieuw-Amsterdam New York werd en hoe zelfs to 1773 Nederlands de officiële taal bleef in het voormalige Nieuw-Nederland. Het is uiteraard wegens tijdsgebrek onmogelijk over de invloed en de evolutie van de Nederlandse taal en kultuur in al deze gebieden te spreken. Daarom stel ik voor uitvoerig te spreken over de teleurgang en opleving van de Nederlandse taal en kultuur in Noord-Frankrijk, een gebied dat bekend staat als Frans-Vlaanderen. Verder zal ik spreken over de ontwikkeling van de Nederlandse taal en kultuur in Centraal en Zuid-Afrika. Deze gebieden heb ik uitgekozen omdat ze volgens mij het antwoord houden op de vraag waarom het Nederlands nooit is uitgegroeid tot een wereldtaal en aldus kan beschouwd worden als de taal van de gemiste kansen. Tenslotte nog dit: in mijn lezing spreek ik niet over Hollanders en Vlamingen, maar wel gebruik ik de termen Noord- en Zuid-Nederlanders omdat ze beter de taaleenheid beschrijven die er altijd heeft bestaan tussen Holland en Vlaanderen.

2. Het Nederlands in Frans-Vlaanderen

Als men Frans-Vlaanderen bezoekt heeft men het gevoel alsof men op bezoek gaat bij verwanten die door een gebrek aan elementaire culturele begeleiding achterop geraakt zijn. Volgens een conservatieve schatting wordt het Nederlands, of beter gezegd een Vlaamse dialectvorm ervan, nu nog gesproken in Frans-Vlaanderen door ongeveer 200,000 mensen. Volgens een progressieve schatting zijn er dat zelfs 400,000. Nu nog is het mogelijk zich in openbare instellingen en winkels met Nederlands te behelpen. Inderdaad, volgens vele getuigenissen wordt, als men er zich in het Nederlands uitdrukt, ontvangen als een oudere broer die men lang niet meer gezien heeft. De ontwikkeling van de Nederlandse taal en kultuur in Frans-Vlaanderen is echter tot voor kort door de Franse autoriteiten op brutale manier onderdrukt. De anti-Nederlandse geschiedenis van dit gebied heeft dan ook tot gevolg gehad dat vele Frans-Vlamingen in een niemandsland leven tusen twee kulturen en nu langzamerhand hun kulturele verbondenheid met de Nederlanden herontdeken.

In de 17de eeuw wilde Frankrijk tijdens de dertigjarige oorlog de Nederlanden inpalmen. Deze aggressieve expansionistische politiek van Frankrijk had tot gevolg dat sinds 1648 vele gebieden van de Zuidelijke Nederlanden door de Fransen werden overrompeld en ingepalmd. Ik noem op: in 1648 werden Atrecht en Bapalmen veroverd. In 1659 was het de beurt van Broekburg en Grevelingen; in 1662, Duinkerken; 1668, St Winoksbergen, Rijsel en Dowaai en na de slag van Kassel in 1677 ook St Omaars, Kamerijk, Kassel, Bavik en Maluize. In 1713 wordt door de vrede van Utrecht de definitieve noordgrens van Frankrijk vastgelegd. Dat betekent dat sinds 1713 de Nederlanden in drie delen zijn gesplitst: de Noordelijke Nederlanden, de Zuidelijke Nederlanden, en Frans-Vlaanderen. Dus sinds 1713 gaat Frans-Vlaanderen zijn eigen weg in een Frans politiek verband en sinds die tijd wordt er de Nederlandse taal en kultuur door de Franse autoriteiten onderdrukt. De verfransing verloopt aanvankelijk traag omdat Frans-Vlaanderen tot 1815 van het bisdom Ieper afhangt. De verfransing maakt echter vlugge vooruitgang in de handel, administratie en leger. De volkstaal blijft echter het Nederlands. De bekende Schrijver Michiel de Swaen leefde en schreef in Duinkerken en stierf er in 1707. Hij schreef nooit een woord in het Frans. De Franse revolutie en de vrij brutale onderdrukking van het Nederlands in de Zuidelijke Nederlanden die erop volgt leidde tot versnelde verfransing van Frans-Vlaanderen dat nu *Le Département du Nord* wordt genoemd. Na de val van Napoléon in 1815 was er een kans om Frans-Vlaanderen terug bij de Zuidelijke Nederlanden aan te hechten. Ik geloof dat in 1815 de Nederlanden een enige kans hebben verkeken om de politieke eenheid van de Nederlanden te herstellen. Het is een feit dat na 1815 het Frans de kultuurtaal wordt in Frans-Vlaanderen; het Vlaams dialect wordt er alleen nog maar gebruikt op de kansel en als volkstaal.

Maar de verfransing gaat eveneens gepaard met een Frans-Vlaamse beweging die er voor ijvert het Nederlands terug te doen aannemen. Zo wordt in 1853 het *Commité Flamand de France* opgericht met als leuze "Moedertaal en vaderland". Af en toe zijn er enkele individuen die de kop opsteken en op vernederlandsing aandringen. Een daarvan is de bekende dichter Guido Gezelle en Charles de Gaulle, de grootoom van de latere President van Frankrijk. Hij zei in 1870: *"La question des langues se posera tôt ou tard"* ("het taalprobleem zal zich vroeg of laat stellen"). Het is spijtig dat de latere President van Frankrijk zich nooit deze verwittiging van zijn grootoom heeft herinnerd of willen herinneren

Tot voor kort was het onderwijs van het Nederlands in Frankrijk bij wet verboden. In 1833 werd the Nederlands formeel als taal verboden en in het bijzonder als onderwijstaal; deze wet werd bekrachtigd in 1882. Frankrijk kon het blijbaar aan Vlaanderen nooit vergeven dat het een hardnekkige strijd had gevoerd om onze onafhandelijkheid te waarborgen. Maar in 1970 werd voor het Nederlands de deur weer op een kiertje gezet. Sinds 1970 mag het Nederlands terug in de scholen onderwezen worden en dat wordt nu ook gedaan in enkele middelbare scholen van Frans-Vlaanderen. Deze ommekeer in de Franse politiek valt samen met de oprichting van het eerste Vlaamse Parlement van België. Met de groeiende politieke macht van Vlaanderen zou men er wel eens kunnen aan denken de activiteiten van de *Alliance Française* in de Zuidelijke Nederlanden af te remmen indien het Nederlands in

Frankrijk nog langer gediscrimineerd wordt.

Sinds de Tweede Wereldoorlog is er eveneens nieuw leven geblazen in de Frans-Vlaamse beweging in Frans-Vlaanderen. En het Vlaamse dialect wordt er in sommige dorpen nog als volkstaal gebruikt. Ik lees een getuigenis voor:

> Zo fungeerde het Vlaams een beetje als geheime taal tussen mijn ouders en de andere volwassenen. Voor alle ernstige zaken spraken de erstige mensen, zelfs onze pastoor en onze kapelaan Vlaams. Het was ook de enige taal die de paarden en de honden kon bedaren! En als de oude mensen met roestige fietsen een potje koffie kwamen drinken om over heden en verleden te klappen ... spraken ze ook onze prachtige vertellerstaal.

Kort na de oorlog, werd er een Komitee voor Frans-Vlaanderen opgericht dat beoogt de Nederlandse bewustwording in Frans-Vlaanderen te bevorderen zodat daar opnieuw leiders kunnen opstaan na de repressiegesel van 1945. Ik geloof dat het de morele plicht is van Noord- en Zuid-Nederland de nodige middelen ter beschikking te stellen om de sociale en culturele ontvoogding van Frans-Vlaanderen door te voeren.

3. De Nederlandse taal en kultuur in Centraal Afrika

Een ander voorbeeld van Frans anti-nederlandsgezindheid en aggressiviteit vindt men in Centraal Afrika, in het bijzonder in de voormalige Belgische Congo, dat nu Zaïre heet. In deze kolonie werden gedurende vele tientallen jaren de kulturele rechten van de Zuid Nederlanders bestreden. "Flamin" was dan ook een scheldwoord dat door de Kongolezen werd gebruikt als een scheldwoord zonder goed te beseffen wat het betekende en zonder te begrijpen dat ze het slachtoffer waren van verstoorde informatie. Het is dan ook niet te verwonderen dat de strijd voor

Nederlandstalig onderwijs in Centraal Afrika langduring en vaak pijnlijk is geweest. Zowel Franstalige Belgen en door anti-Vlaamse opgehitste inboorlingen verzetten zich tegen het leren en het gebruik van het Nederlands. Zo volgden in het schooljaar 1956-57 slechts 2,119 studenten uit een total van 22,567 de Nederlandse klassen. Met de toenemende politieke macht van de Zuidelijke Nederlanden in het Belgische staatsverband werd door Vlaanderen echter meer en meer druk uitgeoefend op de Belgische regering opdat het Nederlands zijn rechtmatige plaats zou krijgen in de kolonie. Zo eiste in 1958 het Vlaamse Economische Verbond gelijke behandeling voor de Nederlandse taal en kultuur. In het bijzonder werd geëist dat Nederlands naast het Frans zou erkend worden als de officiële onderwijstaal van de inboorlingen in het lager onderwijs. De onafhankelijkheid van Zaire in 1960 heeft aan die taalbeweging een voortijdig einde gemaakt: het is de zoveelste gemiste kans van de Nederlandse taal. Sinds 1960 is het onderwijs van de Nederlandse taal in privé-handen overgegaan.

In zo'n klimaat van kulturele aggressie is het dan ook niet te verwonderen dat van 1908 tot 1942 de ontwikkeling van de Nederlandse-Afrikaanse letterkunde en het literair talent in de kiem werden gesmoord. De eerste belangrijke werken over de Belgische kolonie werden geschreven door Noord-Nederlanders, namelijk Van Booven en Vermeulen, en niet door Zuid-Nederlanders! In 1942 werd echter het Nederlandse Literaire Tijdschrift voor Centraal-Afrika gesticht, *De Band*. Zuid-Nederlandse schrijvers, die ondertussen een zekere bekendheid hebben verworven, hebben daarin geschreven, zoals Lodewijk de Lentdecker, Tone Brulin en Jef Geraerts. De belangrijkste schrijver is wel Albert van Hoeck wiens boek, *De rechter en de goeverneur*, werd bekroond voor de 6de Conferentie van de Nederlandse Letteren in Den Haag in 1958.

4. De Nederlandse taal en kultuur in Zuid-Afrika

In 1647 leed het Hollandse schip, Noord-Haarlem, schipbreuk in de Tafelbaai in Zuid-Afrika. Toen de schipbreukelingen terug in Holland waren, overtuigden ze de Oostindische Compagnie er een blijvende Hollandse nederzetting op te richten. In 1651 werd Jan van Riebeeck, een 31-jarige dokter belast er een blijvende militaire vestiging te bouwen. Op 6 april van dat jaar zette hij, met drie schepen uitgevaren, voet aan wal. Hij was vergezeld van zijn echtgenote, Maria de la Queillerie en familieleden. Van Riebeeck werd opgevolgd door Simon van der Stel. In het begin van de 18de eeuw leefden er ongeveer 2000 immigranten in de kolonie. De meeste immigranten kwamen uit Zuid-Holland en Zeeland: er kwamen Frans-Vlamingen en Duitsers bij. Uit deze smeltkroes onstond het Afrikaanse volk en zijn Afrikaanse spreektaal. In de kolonie bleef de Nederlandse bouwtrant domineren en het calvinisme bleef er de officiële godsdienst.

Gedurende 143 jaar bleef de Kaap een Hollandse kolonie. In 1795 bezetten de Engelsen het gebied. Maar de Zuid-Afrikanen hadden ondertussen een nationaal gevoel ontwikkeld en ze roepen daarop de Bataafse republiek uit. Uiteindelijk trokken ze aan het korste eind en met have en goed gingen ze per ossewagen op zoek naar een nieuw land waar ze naar eigen aard konden leven. Dat was de Grote Trek (1835-1843) die leidde tot de stichting van twee onafhankelijke boerenrepublieken, Transvaal en Oranje-Vrijstaat, maar Kaapland en Natal bleven onder Engels bewind. Toen echter goud en diamant werden ontdekt in de boeren republieken brak de eerste boerenoorlog uit met de Engelsen in 1895-96 en een tweede beslissende oorlog van 1899 tot 1902. Tijdens de boerenoorlogen sympatiseerde Noord- en Zuid-Nederland met de boeren maar het werd een ongelijke strijd. De Engelsen hadden overmacht aan manschappen en wapens. De Engelsen pasten de taktiek van de verschroeide aarde toe. Vee werd afgeslacht, vrouwen en kinderen werden in concentratiekampen gestopt, 26,000 mensen stierven aan ontbering, marteling en ziekte. President Kruger moest vluchten en werd door het Nederlandse oorlogsschip, Gelderland, dat door Koningin Wilhelmina overhaast was gestuurd, in triomf naar Europa gebracht. De Zuid-Afrikaanse boeren waren wel militair verslagen maar het Zuid-Afrikaanse nationalisme had een nieuwe stuwkracht gekregen en daarover zal ik straks meer vertellen. Op 31 mei 1910 werd de grondwet van de Unie van Zuid-Afrika afgekondigd. De vroegere boerengeneraal Botha slaagde erin de vier provinciën tot een eenheid samen te voegen en in 1913 werd reeds de weg van apartheid opgegaan. In 1929 benoemde Zuid-Afrika haar eerste ambassadeur in het buitenland en dat was in Nederland. Op 31 mei 1961 tenslotte werd de Republiek van Zuid-Afrika uitgeroepen en "Die Stem van Sud-Afrika" werd het nationale volkslied.

Zoals ik reeds zei waren de meeste immigranten in de tweede helft van de 17de eeuw afkomstig uit Zuid-Holland en Zeeland. De enige band met de Nederlandse taal gebeurde via de bijbel en de omgangstaal begon spoedig af the wijken van het Nederlands. De gesproken taal was een vereenvoudiging van de Nederlandse taal en alleen in de kerk werd het hooghollands gebruikt. Toen echter tegen het einde van de 18de eeuw de Engelsen Zuid-Afrika begonnen te koloniseren, trachtte het Engels het Afrikaans en het Nederlands te verdringen. Als reactie onstond daarop de eerste Afrikaanse taalbeweging die echer werd gekortwiekt door de Engelsen. In een getuigenis van 1875 wordt gezegd:

> Wie zich niet laat angliseren wordt uitgescholden. Het spreken van de engelse taal: dat is vooruitgang zo roepen de schreeuwers, dat is beschaving, die dat niet geloven wil is ouderwets en dom.

De Afrikaanse taalbeweging werd niet alleen maar gedoodverfd door de Engelsen maar ook door diegenen die mooi Nederlands spraken. Ze beschreven het Afrikaans als een verminkt en gebrekkig Nederlands, goed voor onbeschaafden, maar ongeschikt als kultuurtaal.

In 1875 werd door Du Toit *Die Genootskap van Regte Afrikaners* opgericht met als doel het Afrikaans als schrijftaal te doen erkennen naast het Nederlands en het Engels. In het begin van de 20ste eeuw onstond een tweede Afrikaanse taalbeweging. Het Nederlands werd teruggedrongen tot boekentaal. Het Afrikaans werd nu ook gesteund door zijn ontluikende letterkunde en de verdere evolutie verliep verrrassend snel. In 1914 werd het Afrikaans de voertaal in de scholen en in 1925 werd de grondwet in het Afrikaans vertaald. Dus: de boeren werden in de boerenoorlogen wel verslagen door de Engelsen maar daardoor groeide het Afrikaanse nationalisme en doorzettingsvermogen waardoor tenslotte het Afrikaans een morele en kulturele overwinning behaalde op de Engelsen. Nu is het Afrikaans allang als een zelfstandige en volwassen taal erkend, die nauw met het Nederlands verwant is. Het Afrikaans is in het Parlement en administratie de voertaal. De afkeer tegenover het Engelse kultuurexpansionisme heeft als gevolg gehad de ontvoogding van het Afrikaans waardoor alle vreemde talen, met uitzondering van het Nederlands zoveel mogelijk worden geweerd. Nieuwe Nederlandse woorden daarentegen worden aangepast aan de Afrikaanse taalvorm en worden als een verrijking van de taal beschouwd. Door het taalpuritanisme is het Afrikaans dikwijls zuiverder dan het Nederlands. Terwijl veel vreemde woorden in het Nederlands worden opgenomen, gebeurt dit zelden in het Afrikaans. Enkele voorbeelden:

> prikkelpop (pin-up)
>
> Appetijtwekkertje (aperitif)

Moltrein (metro)

Vuurhoutje (lucifer)

Het Afrikaans is nu de moedertaal van 60% der blanken en 90% der kleurlingen. Het grote probleem voor de Afrikaanse taal is het doorbreken van het geestelijk isolement en de afscheiding van het Westen. Het Nederlands en het Afrikaans zijn zeer verwante kultuurgemeenschappen en er wordt gedaan aan kulturele uitwisseling en samenwerking. Zo startte de staatsbibliotheek van Pretoria met een grote schenking van Nederlandse boeken uit Leiden en Antwerpen.

5. De reden waarom het Nederlands de taal is van de gemiste kansen

Ik geloof, nu wij deze geschiedenis hebben doorgemaakt dat we een afdoend antwoord kunnen geven op de vraag waarom het Nederlands nooit is uitgegroeid tot een feitelijke wereldtaal alhoewel de taal een toegangspoort is tot een veelomvattende kultureel erfgoed. Een van de redenen is dat de volksgemeenschap van de Nederlanden nooit bezeten is geweest door veroveringszucht. Nooit heeft zij, opgezweept door een expansionistische ideologie, een gemeenschap aangevallen. Het was dan ook eerder gemakkelijk voor andere volkeren, die door veroveringzucht bezeten waren om die Nederlandse bruggehoofden uit te schakelen.

Zo was het Nederlands bijna een wereldtaal geworden in Europa, maar Frankrijk als een niet aflatende hebzuchtige stak stokken in de wielen. Frankrijk had gehoopt de Nederlanden te kunnen inlijven. Frans-Vlaanderen heeft als een soort buffergebied de grote stoot opgevangen. Het is een offer dat wij, Nooord- en Zuid Nederlanders nooit mogen vergeten. Indien Frans-Vlaanderen een deel was gebleven van de Zuidelijke Nederlanden, dan zou nu het Nederlands door 4 miljoen meer mensen gesproken worden. Door de politieke verhoudingen tussen Frankrijk en de Zuidelijke Nederlanden werd door Frankrijk en de ganse Franssprekende wereld een Grendel gezet op de poort naar de Nederlanden en het onderwijs van de Nederlandse taal werd verboden. In Centraal Afrika kreeg het Nederlands geen kans omdat er toen een anti-Vlaams bewind was in België. In Zuid-Afrika zijn het de Engelsen geweest die roet in het eten hebben gegooid toen de Nederlandse taal aan het doorbreken was. Een tweede reden waarom het Nederlands nooit tot een echte wereldtaal is uitgegroeid is dat, in tegenstelling tot andere naties, de Noordelijke Nederlanden nooit de Nederlandse taal aan de inboorlingen hebben opgedrongen. Zo was het in Nederlands-Indië (Indonesië), Ceylon en in de Nederlandse Antillen. Een derde reden is dat de Noordelijke en Zuidelijke Nederlanden hun immigranten die uitweken op een onvoldoende wijze kultureel hebben begeleid. Zo was het mogelijk dat het Nederlands door het Afrikaans in Zuid-Afrika tot boekentaal werd teruggedrongen.

Hoe komt het dat het Nederlands door anderstaligen zo weinig is gekend? Natuurlijk ligt dat aan het geringe economische belang van onze taal, maar het is ongetwijfeld ook te wijten aan de verwarring, vooroordelen en onzekerheid, gebrekkige informatie en vijandigheid tegenover de Nederlandse kultuur. Bijvoorbeeld, het is spijtig dat sinds het verdrag van Westfalen in 1648 er in het buitenland onduidelijkheid is onstaan rond de begrippen "Hollands", "Nederlands" en "Vlaams". Sinsdien weten nog maar weinigen in het buitenland dat de Noordelijke en Zuidelijke Nederlanden altijd een taaleenheid hebben gevormd en tijdens de laatste 30 jaar ook een kultuurgemeenshap aan het worden is.

De fout ligt niet alleen aan de anderstaligen maar ook aan de

Noord- en Zuid-Nederlanders die het spreken van een andere taal blijkbaar een statussymbool vinden. Onlangs werd nog voorgesteld in het Europese Parlement de onmiddellijke vertaling van de debatten in het Nederlands niet toe te laten omdat verondersteld wordt dat alle Nederlandssprekende afgevaardigden toch Engels kunnen spreken. Het is noodzakelijk de mogelijkheden die nu geboden worden door de Europese instellingen om het gebruik en het onderwijs van het Nederlands te stimuleren, ook te gebruiken. Een gebrek aan zelfliefde zou wel eens het begin kunnen zijn van een langzame dood van onze kultuur.

Het Nederlands is dus wel de taal van de gemiste kansen maar dat is nog geen reden om triestig te zijn want gezien de moeizame en steeds belaagde groei van het Nederlands, zowel in en buiten de Nederlanden, is het een taal die net zogoed niet had kunnen bestaan.

About the Author

Professor Gabriël A. Moens AM is Emeritus Professor of Law, The University of Queensland. He served as Pro Vice Chancellor, Dean and Professor of Law, Murdoch University; Head, Graduate School of Law, The University of Notre Dame Australia; Garrick Professor of Law, The University of Queensland; and Professor of Law, Curtin University. He was a Visiting Professor of Law at J. Reuben Clark Law School, Brigham Young University and at Loyola University, New Orleans.

He is the Founder and Emeritus Editor-in-Chief of International Trade and Business Law Review. In 1999, Professor Moens received the Australian Award for University Teaching in Law and Legal Studies. In 2003, the Prime Minister of Australia awarded him the Australian Centenary Medal for services to education. He was named the "International Alumnus of the Year" by the Pritzker Law School of Northwestern University in 2019. In June 2019 he was appointed a Member of the Order of Australia (AM) for services to the law and higher education. Professor Moens is a Membre Titulaire, International Academy of Comparative Law, Paris; a Fellow of the Australian Institute of Management (WA); a Fellow of the College of Law; and a Fellow of the Australian Academy of Law.

He is co-author/co-editor of *The Himalaya Clause*, Connor Court Publishing, 2020; *Law of International Business in Australasia* (2nd ed), The Federation Press, 2019; *The Constitution of the Commonwealth of Australia Annotated* (9th ed), LexisNexis Butterworths, 2016; *Arbitration and Dispute Resolution in the Resources Sector: An Australian Perspective*, Springer, 2015; *Jurisprudence of Liberty* (2nd ed), LexisNexis, 2011; *Commercial Law of the European Union*, Springer, 2010; and *International Trade and Business: Law, Policy and Ethics* (2nd ed), Routledge/Cavendish, 2006. In 2020 Boolarong Press published Gabriêl's debut novel, *A Twisted Choice*.

Also Available

A COMMITMENT TO EXCELLENCE

Essays in Honour of Emeritus Professor Gabriël A. Moens

Edited by Augusto Zimmermann

Paperback, 495 pages, $49.95
October 2018
ISBN: 9781925826203
Available from www.connorcourtpublishing.com.au

Emeritus Professor Gabriël A. Moens is a prominent Australian academic, researcher, teacher and administrator and his legacy is nothing short of extraordinary. Over his long and distinguished career he has acquired a solid reputation as a leading academic expert in constitutional law, legal philosophy, and business law, in particular in its international and comparative dimensions.

Edited by Professor Augusto Zimmermann, 'A Commitment to Excellence: Essays in Honour of Professor Gabriël A. Moens' is a collection of essays written by leading lawyers and academics who share a profound admiration for his extraordinary life and legacy. These essays address some of the topics Professor Moens has taught during his highly successful career. These include constitutional law, contract law, comparative law, jurisprudence, European Union law, International commercial law, trade law, arbitration law and practice, and mooting.

The result is a deeply impressive collection of articles that is a most fitting tribute to the remarkable career of Professor Moens.

Lightning Source UK Ltd.
Milton Keynes UK
UKHW040954300621
386394UK00001B/59